Turgene

A Study

Edward Garnett

Alpha Editions

This edition published in 2024

ISBN : 9789362519641

Design and Setting By
Alpha Editions
www.alphaedis.com
Email - info@alphaedis.com

As per information held with us this book is in Public Domain.
This book is a reproduction of an important historical work. Alpha Editions uses the best technology to reproduce historical work in the same manner it was first published to preserve its original nature. Any marks or number seen are left intentionally to preserve its true form.

FOREWORD

DEAR EDWARD—I am glad to hear that you are about to publish a study of Turgenev, that fortunate artist who has found so much in life for us and no doubt for himself, with the exception of bare justice. Perhaps that will come to him, too, in time. Your study may help the consummation. For his luck persists after his death. What greater luck an artist like Turgenev could wish for than to find in the English-speaking world a translator who has missed none of the most delicate, most simple beauties of his work, and a critic who has known how to analyse and point out its high qualities with perfect sympathy and insight.

After twenty odd years of friendship (and my first literary friendship too) I may well permit myself to make that statement, while thinking of your wonderful Prefaces as they appeared from time to time in the volumes of Turgenev's complete edition, the last of which came into the light of public indifference in the ninety-ninth year of the nineteenth century.

With that year one may say, with some justice, that the age of Turgenev had come to an end too; only work so simple and human, so independent of the transitory formulas and theories of art belongs as you point out in the Preface to *Smoke* "to all time."

Turgenev's creative activity covers about thirty years. Since it came to an end the social and political events in Russia have moved at an accelerated pace, but the deep origins of them, in the moral and intellectual unrest of the souls, are recorded in the whole body of his work with the unerring lucidity of a great national writer. The first stirrings, the first gleams of the great forces can be seen almost in every page of the novels, of the short stories and of *A Sportsman's Sketches*—those marvellous landscapes peopled by unforgettable figures.

Those will never grow old. Fashions in monsters do change, but the truth of humanity goes on for ever, unchangeable and inexhaustible in the variety of its disclosures. Whether Turgenev's art, which has captured it with such mastery and such gentleness, is for "all time" it is hard to say. Since, as you say yourself, he brings all his problems and characters to the test of love we may hope that it will endure at least till the infinite emotions of love are replaced by the exact simplicity of perfected Eugenics. But even by then, I think, women would not have changed much; and the women of Turgenev who understood them so tenderly, so reverently and so passionately—they, at least, are certainly for all time.

Women are, one may say, the foundation of his art. They are Russian of course. Never was a writer so profoundly, so whole-souledly national. But for non-Russian readers, Turgenev's Russia is but a canvas on which the incomparable artist of humanity lays his colours and his forms in the great light and the free air of the world. Had he invented them all and also every stick and stone, brook and hill and field in which they move, his personages would have been just as true and as poignant in their perplexed lives. They are his own and also universal. Any one can accept them with no more question than one accepts the Italians of Shakespeare.

In the larger non-Russian view, what should make Turgenev sympathetic and welcome to the English-speaking world, is his essential humanity. All his creations, fortunate and unfortunate, oppressed and oppressors are human beings, not strange beasts in a menagerie or damned souls knocking themselves about in the stuffy darkness of mystical contradictions. They are human beings, fit to live, fit to suffer, fit to struggle, fit to win, fit to lose, in the endless and inspiring game of pursuing from day to day the ever-receding future.

I began by calling him lucky, and he was, in a sense. But one ends by having some doubts. To be so great without the slightest parade and so fine without any tricks of "cleverness" must be fatal to any man's influence with his contemporaries.

Frankly, I don't want to appear as qualified to judge of things Russian. It wouldn't be true. I know nothing of them. But I am aware of a few general truths, such as, for instance, that no man, whatever may be the loftiness of his character, the purity of his motives and the peace of his conscience—no man, I say, likes to be beaten with sticks during the greater part of his existence. From what one knows of his history it appears clearly that in Russia almost any stick was good enough to beat Turgenev with in his latter years. When he died the characteristically chicken-hearted Autocracy hastened to stuff his mortal envelope into the tomb it refused to honour, while the sensitive Revolutionists went on for a time flinging after his shade those jeers and curses from which that impartial lover of *all* his countrymen had suffered so much in his lifetime. For he, too, was sensitive. Every page of his writing bears its testimony to the fatal absence of callousness in the man.

And now he suffers a little from other things. In truth it is not the convulsed terror-haunted Dostoevski but the serene Turgenev who is under a curse. For only think! Every gift has been heaped on his cradle: absolute sanity and the deepest sensibility, the clearest vision and the quickest responsiveness, penetrating insight and unfailing generosity of judgment, an exquisite perception of the visible world and an unerring instinct for the significant, for the essential in the life of men and women, the clearest mind, the warmest heart, the largest sympathy—and all that in perfect measure. There's enough there to ruin the prospects of any writer. For you know very well, my dear Edward, that if you had Antinous himself in a booth of the world's-fair, and killed yourself in protesting that his soul was as perfect as his body, you wouldn't get one per cent of the crowd struggling next door for a sight of the Double-headed Nightingale or of some weak-kneed giant grinning through a horse collar.—Yours,

J. C.

INTRODUCTORY NOTE

For permission to use certain Prefaces, which I wrote originally for my wife's Translations of the Novels and Tales of Ivan Turgenev, and for the use of a few quotations from her versions I have to thank Mr. William Heinemann, the publisher of the Collected Edition.

E. G.

March 1917.

I
TURGENEV'S CRITICS AND HIS DETRACTORS

CHAPTER I

TURGENEV'S CRITICS AND HIS DETRACTORS

A writer, Mr. Robert Lynd, has said: "It is the custom when praising a Russian writer to do so at the expense of all other Russian writers. It is as though most of us were monotheists in our devotion to authors, and could not endure to see any respect paid to the images of the rivals of the gods of the moment. And so one year Tolstoy is laid prone as Dagon, and another year, Turgenev. And no doubt the day will come when Dostoevsky will fall from his huge eminence."

One had hoped that the disease, long endemic in Russia, of disparaging Turgenev, would not have spread to England, but some enthusiastic explorers of things Russian came back home with a mild virus and communicated the spores of the misunderstanding. That misunderstanding, dating at least fifty years back, was part of the polemics of the rival Russian political parties. The Englishman who finds it strange that Turgenev's pictures of contemporary Russian life should have excited such angry heat and raised such clouds of acrimonious smoke may imagine the fate of a great writer in Ireland to-day who should go on his way serenely, holding the balance level between the Unionists, the Nationalists, the Sinn Féin, the people of Dublin, and the people of Belfast. The more impartial were his pictures as art, the louder would rise the hubbub that his types were "exceptional," that his insight was "limited," that he did not understand either the politicians or the gentry or the peasants, that he had not fathomed all that was in each "movement," that he was palming off on us heroes who had "no real existence." And, in the sense that Turgenev's serene and beautiful art excludes thousands of aspects that filled the newspapers and the minds of his contemporaries, his detractors have reason.

Various Russian critics, however, whom Mr. Maurice Baring, and a French biographer, M. Haumant, have echoed, have gone further, and in their critical ingenuity have mildly damned the Russian master's creations. It seems to these gentlemen that there is a great deal of water in Turgenev's wine. Mr. Baring tells us that Tolstoy and Dostoevsky "reached the absolute truth of the life which was round them," and that "people are beginning to ask themselves whether Turgenev's pictures are true (!), whether the Russians that he describes ever existed, and whether the praise which was bestowed upon him by his astonished contemporaries all over Europe was not a gross exaggeration."

> "Turgenev painted people of the same epoch, the same generation; he dealt with the same material; he dealt with it as an artist and as a poet, as a great artist and a great poet.

But his vision was weak and narrow compared with that of Tolstoy, and his understanding was cold and shallow compared with that of Dostoevsky. His characters beside those of Tolstoy seem caricatures, and beside those of Dostoevsky they are conventional.... When all is said, Turgenev was a great poet. What time has not taken away from him, and what time can never take away, is the beauty of his language and the poetry in his work.... Turgenev never wrote anything better than the book which brought him fame, the *Sportsman's Sketches*. In this book nearly the whole of his talent finds expression.

"No one can deny that the characters of Turgenev live; they are intensely vivid. Whether they are true to life is another question. The difference between the work of Tolstoy and Turgenev is this: that Turgenev's characters are as living as any characters are in books, but they belong, comparatively speaking, to bookland and are thus conventional; whereas Tolstoy's characters belong to life. The fault which Russian critics find with Turgenev's characters is that they are exaggerated, that there is an element of caricature in them, and that they are permeated by the faults of the author's own character, namely, his weakness, and, above all, his self-consciousness.

"... Than Bazarov there is no character in the whole of his work which is more alive ... (but he is) a book-character, extraordinarily vivid and living though he be.... Dostoevsky's Nihilists, however outwardly fantastic they may seem, are inwardly not only truer, but the very quintessence of truth.... (*Virgin Soil*) Here in the opinion of all Russian judges, and of most latter-day judges who have knowledge of the subject, he failed. In describing the official class, although he does this with great skill and cleverness, he makes a gallery of caricatures; and the revolutionaries whom he sets before us as types, however good they may be as fiction, are not the real thing.

"The lapse of years has only emphasized the elements of banality—and conventionality—which are to be found in Turgenev's work. He is a masterly landscape painter; but even here he is not without convention. His landscapes are always orthodox Russian landscapes, and are seldom varied.

> He seems never to get face to face with nature, after the manner of Wordsworth; he never gives us any elemental pictures of nature, such as Gorky succeeds in doing in a phrase; but he rings the changes on delicate arrangements of wood, cloud, mist, and water, vague backgrounds and diaphanous figures, after the manner of Corot."—*Landmarks in Russian Literature*, pp. 99-110.

It is obvious from the above criticisms of Mr. Baring and the Russian critics whom he represents that what is the matter with Turgenev in their eyes is his "vision," his "temperament." They admire his language, his beautiful style: they pay lip service to him as "a poet." They even admit that he was "a great artist," but they do not suspect that his intellectual pre-eminence is disguised from them by his very aesthetic qualities, balance, contrast, grouping, perspective, harmony of form and perfect modelling, qualities in which Turgenev not only far surpasses Tolstoy and Dostoevsky, but any nineteenth-century European. Further, it is evident that these critics, having themselves never seen or felt in nature's life those shades of "truth" which Turgenev's poetical vision reveals to us, imagine that such have no "real" existence! Otherwise these critics would have laid stress on these special shades and tones and not passed them by with a perfunctory nod. One may go further and assert that it is precisely this same "poetic vision" which irritates Turgenev's detractors; they resent it, because it conflicts with the more prosaic, everyday point of view. They mean by "truth" something both more photographic and commonplace, something more striking or more ordinary in the "lighting," something observed with less beautiful shades of feeling, less exquisitely stamped and recorded in classical contours.

Let us examine some of these charges. "Turgenev's characters are as living as any in books, but they belong, comparatively speaking, to bookland, and are thus conventional." But why *conventional*? Why damn all the great creations in *books*, from Don Quixote downwards, as bookish? Are Turgenev's women characters, say Maria Nikolaevna, Zinaïda, Varvara Pavlovna, Irene, Elena, Anna Martinovna, creations which are more highly individualized than are Tolstoy's women, conventional? No more than are Shakespeare's women, Lady Macbeth, Imogen, Juliet, Beatrice, Desdemona, Portia. Mr. Baring cannot mean this absurdity. But he repeats the charge "Bazarov is a 'book-character,' extraordinarily vivid and living though he be," evidently thinking that because Bazarov is a figure synthesizing social tendencies and a mental attitude peculiar to his time, he is inferior as a creation to, say, Tolstoy's Vronsky. On the contrary, that is why Bazarov is both psychologically and humanly a much more interesting figure, and one higher in the creative scale than Vronsky. Nature denied Tolstoy the power of constructing a Rudin or a Bazarov. It is because these types are personifications incarnate of tendencies, traits, and a special mode of thought and action of a particular period, and yet are brimming with individual life, that they are *sui generis, and are irreplaceable creations*. This is Turgenev's glory. We have only to compare Rudin or Bazarov with such heroes as Lermontov's Petchorin or Herzen's Beltoff to recognize that while these latter have all the force of autobiography, they are not shown us in the round. Mr. Baring has been seduced, one imagines, by our generation's preference for the "photographic likeness" in art, which nevertheless, at critical moments, often leaves us in the air: for example, the scene of Vronsky's attempted suicide in *Anna Karenin*. Turgenev could never have been guilty of this piece of banal, doubtful psychology. And the latter-day school of Russian critics, when they ask with Mr. Baring, "Did men ever meet the double of a Bazarov or a Rudin in flesh and in blood? if not, then these characters are bookishly exaggerated or have an element of caricature in them," may be asked in reply, "Did you ever meet Dostoevsky's Alyosha or Prince Myshkin walking and talking in life?" Again, are not three-fourths of Dostoevsky's people permeated by "the faults of the author's own character"? Do they not behave extravagantly or fantastically in a manner all their own? Is there not a strong element of caricature in them? Of course there is, and Mr. Baring and his Russian critics delight in it, and for that very reason exalt Dostoevsky above Turgenev. They exalt the exaggerated Satanic element in Dostoevsky's work, even while they declare "Dostoevsky's Nihilists are not only truer than Turgenev's, but the *very quintessence of truth*"! We are more humble in our claims for Nezhdanov and Marianna and Mashurina in *Virgin Soil*; we do not assert that they are "the very quintessence of truth"; but we know that these creations are not "caricatures" in the sense that Stepan Trofimovitch and Karmazinov in *The Possessed* are caricatures. We know, on the contrary, that Turgenev's Nihilists, in Kropotkin's words, are real representatives of "the very earliest phases of the movement…. Turgenev had, with his wonderful intuition, caught some of the most striking features of the movement, viz. the early promoters' 'Hamletism,' and their misconception of the peasantry." How curious it is that Stepniak and Kropotkin, who themselves lived with and knew intimately these early Nihilists, bear witness to the truth of Turgenev's portraiture, while MM. Baring and Brückner and Haumant, these critics of our own generation, tell us "Turgenev's Nihilists are not the real thing"! While admitting that Turgenev had his comparative failures, such as Insarov in *On the Eve*, one observes that Turgenev's detractors demand from his social pictures what they demand from no other of his contemporaries, "the whole objective truth and nothing but the truth." And this curious demand, fundamentally at the root of the widespread misunderstanding about Turgenev's work, has been spread and caught up and re-echoed by the great tribe of partisan critics, political propagandists, Slavophils, reactionaries, progressives, for two generations. Necessarily Turgenev, this consummate artist whose contemporary pictures synthesize many aspects of the social and political movements of his time, colours and tones his work with his own personality, as do all the other great creators. Just as the hero, Olenin in *The Cossacks*, Levin in *Anna Karenin*, and Pierre in *War and Peace*, are projections of Tolstoy's individuality, so Lavretski, Litvinov, Sanin, and other characters, are projections of Turgenev's personality. It is the same with Fielding, with Balzac and Maupassant, with Dostoevsky and Gontcharov, whose characters also "are compacted of the result of their observation, with all their own inner feelings, their loves and hates, their anger and disdain." But only in Turgenev's case, it appears, it is a sin that the creations should contain a certain amount of "subjective reality." It must therefore be the case that it is precisely Turgenev's "temperament" which is at fault in the eyes of critics who assert that "his vision was weak and narrow compared with that of Tolstoy, and his understanding was cold and shallow compared with that of Dostoevsky." How curious that the vision which created *Fathers and Children* and *The Poems in Prose* should have been relatively weak and narrow! and that the understanding which created *A House of Gentlefolk* and *A Sportsman's Sketches* should have been cold and shallow! And yet in the same breath we are instructed that Turgenev "dealt with his generation as a great poet and a great artist." A great poet with a relatively weak and narrow vision, a great artist with a relatively cold and shallow understanding! This is an enigma to us, but not to Turgenev's detractors.

No! One must fall back on other explanations of Turgenev's comparative unpopularity. The first is that beauty of form, a master's sense of composition, an exquisite feeling for balance are less and less prized in modern opinion. Our age has turned its back on the masters possessed of these classic qualities. Modern life flows along congested roads, and modern art responds in bewilderment to an embarrassment of forces. Corot's example in painting is no longer extolled save by the true connoisseur. The grace of beauty is more or less out of fashion. The wider becomes the circle of modern readers and the more the audience enfolds the great bourgeois class, the less are form, clarity and beauty prized. The second explanation is that the inspiration of Love, and the range of exquisite feelings of Love, so manifest in Turgenev's vision, are slightly *vieux jeu*. When Dostoevsky is sentimental, as in *The Insulted and Injured*, he turns one's stomach. It is impossible to read him, so false, exaggerated and unreal are his characters' emotions. But when Turgenev is sentimental, as he is in passages in *The Diary of a Superfluous Man*, *A Correspondence*, *Faust*, one finds oneself to be in the atmosphere of a faded drawing-room of the "'forties." This perishable element undoubtedly exists in some of Turgenev's short stories: it was the heritage he received from the Romantic movement of his fathers, and occasionally, here and there, streaks of this romanticism appear and are detrimental to the firm and delicate objectivity of his creations. But, apart from the question of these streaks of sentimentalism, it is obvious that Turgenev in his attitude towards love and women is nearer to Shakespeare than is, say, Tchehov. Liza and Elena are almost as far removed from the range of our modern creators as are Imogen and Desdemona. It is not that we do not believe firmly in their existence, but that the changed social atmosphere of our times does not so sharply develop and outline woman's spiritual characteristics: such heroines are now free to act in many directions denied to Turgenev's heroines. A girl might say, to-day, of Elena, "Grandmother was like that! so father says, and grandfather saw her like that! Isn't it interesting?" And this change in our social atmosphere, undoubtedly, is a bar to Turgenev's popularity in the eyes of the younger generation.

Again, despite the change of fashion in schools of landscape painters, it is amusing to hear that Turgenev—"this masterly landscape painter"—is charged with "never getting face to face with nature, after the manner of Wordsworth—and Gorky"! But Mr. Baring is echoing his French authority, M. Haumant, who in turn is modestly echoing, it would seem, MM. Mihaïlovsky and Strahov.[1] These eminent authorities on nature are agreed in comparing Turgenev with Corot, "whose subjects and methods scarcely alter." Vogüé, who knew the province of Orel, Turgenev's country, however, does not agree. He says pointedly, "One has to live in the country described by Turgenev to admire how on every page he corroborates our personal impressions, how he brings back to our soul every emotion experienced, and to our senses every subtle odour breathed in that country." This seems explicit.

[1] *Tourguénief, la vie et l'œuvre.* Par Émile Haumant. Paris, 1906.

Never getting face to face with nature! Could a more baseless charge have been made, one falsified by the innermost spirit of Turgenev's work, and by countless passages in his writings, of the most intimate observation?[2] We cite a specimen from *A Tour in the Forest*, showing the penetrating freshness and warmth of his description:

> "I fed my horses, and I too was ferried over. After struggling for a couple of miles through the boggy prairie, I got at last on to a narrow raised wooden causeway to a clearing in the forest. The cart jolted unevenly over the round beams of the causeway; I got out and went along on foot. The horses moved in step, snorting and shaking their heads from the gnats and flies. The forest took us into its bosom. On the outskirts, nearer to the prairie, grew birches, aspens, limes, maples, and oaks. Then they met us more rarely. The dense firwood moved down on us in an unbroken wall. Further on were the red, bare trunks of

pines, and then again a stretch of mixed copse, overgrown with underwood of hazelnut, mountain ash, and bramble, and stout, vigorous weeds. The sun's light threw a brilliant light on the tree-tops, and, filtering through the branches, here and there reached the ground in pale streaks and patches. Birds I scarcely heard—they do not like great forests. Only from time to time there came the doleful and thrice-repeated call of a hoopoe, and the angry screech of a nut-hatch or a jay; a silent, always a solitary bird kept fluttering across the clearing, with a flash of golden azure from its lovely feathers. At times the trees grew further apart, ahead of us the light broke in, the cart came out on a cleared, sandy, open space. Thin rye was growing over it in rows, noiselessly nodding its pale ears. On one side there was a dark, dilapidated little chapel with a slanting cross over a well. An unseen brook was bubbling peacefully with changing, ringing sounds, as though it were flowing into an empty bottle. And then suddenly the road was cut in half by a birch-tree recently fallen, and the forest stood around, so old, lofty and slumbering, that the air seemed pent in. In places the clearing lay under water. On both sides stretched a forest bog, all green and dark, all covered with reeds and tiny alders. Ducks flew up in pairs, and it was strange to see those water-birds darting rapidly about among the pines. 'Ga, ga, ga, ga,' their drawn-out call kept rising unexpectedly. Then a shepherd drove a flock through the underwood; a brown cow with short, pointed horns broke noisily through the bushes, and stood stock-still at the edge of the clearing, her big dark eyes fixed on the dog running before me. A slight breeze brought the delicate pungent smell of burnt wood. A white smoke in the distance crept in eddying rings over the pale, blue forest air, showing that a peasant was charcoal-burning for a glass-factory or for a foundry. The further we went on, the darker and stiller it became all round us. In the pine-forest it is always still; there is only, high overhead, a sort of prolonged murmur and subdued roar in the tree tops.... One goes on and on, and this eternal murmur of the forest never ceases, and the heart gradually begins to sink, and a man longs to come out quickly into the open, into the daylight; he longs to draw a full breath again, and is oppressed by the pungent damp and decay."—*A Tour in the Forest*, pp. 105-107.

[2] "Their predecessors had lived more or less with Nature, but had always looked upon her as something foreign to themselves, with an existence separated from theirs. In Tourguéniev's case this external intercourse becomes a fusion, a mutual pervasion. He feels and recognizes portions of his own being in the wind that shakes the trees, in the light that beams on surrounding objects...."—*A History of Russian Literature*, by K. Waliszewski, p. 290.

Anybody who has lived amid forests and woods must agree that in the passage above Turgenev has seized with unerring exactitude the character, the breath itself of a great woodland, and similarly all his descriptions of nature in *A Sportsman's Sketches* are inspired by profound sensitiveness and close fidelity. "Vague backgrounds and diaphanous figures!" This is the accusation of townsmen.

Another and more insidious line of critical detraction has been followed by M. Haumant in *Ivan Tourguénief, la vie et l'œuvre*, a volume, painstaking and well documented, assuredly of great interest to the student. Intent on his efforts to track down to their source "the origins of Turgenev's thoughts," the French critic has forgotten to applaud the aesthetic appeal, and the very perfection of these creations! It is as though a critic of Keats, in trying to discover "the sources" of "Hyperion" or "An Ode to a Grecian Urn," had neglected to appraise the imperishable essence of these masterpieces. Thus M. Haumant, searching profoundly for "echoes" in Turgenev's "inner voices," gravely informs us that in *The Brigadier* Turgenev has constructed "a Russian Werther"! while a passage in *Phantoms*, it appears, is inspired by a passage in De Quincey's *Confessions of an Opium-Eater*. A page is devoted to the discussion of the latter conjecture,[3] but nothing at all is said as to the unique spiritual beauty and the haunting atmosphere of these tales. And *A Lear of the Steppes*, that masterpiece, incomparable in its force of genius, is dismissed in half a line! The effect of such "comments," both on those who know and those who do not know their Turgenev, is equally unfortunate. For it really looks, but of course one may be wrong, as though the French critic, like his latter-day Russian *confrères*, did not recognize a masterpiece when he sees one. Has not, indeed, a Russian literary teacher, A. D. Alfyorov, publicly declared that "Turgenev's work is, of course, only of historical importance."

[3] Haumant, p. 174.

But enough! Indeed one may well be asked, Is it necessary to defend so great a classic as Turgenev against modern criticisms of this character? Perhaps it is not a mere waste of time, for certain reasons. Turgenev's supremacy, as artist, accepted by the *élite* in France, Renan, Taine, Flaubert, Maupassant, etc., and by the best European critics, such as Brandes, was impaired in Russian eyes by his growing unpopularity after 1867. Brückner says justly:

> "To the intelligent Russian, without a free press, without liberty of assembly, without the right to free expression of opinion, literature became the last refuge of his freedom of thought, the only means of propagating higher ideas. He expected and demanded of his country's literature not merely aesthetic recreation; he placed it at the service of everything noble and good, of his aspiration, of the enlightenment and emancipation of the spirit. *Hence the striking partiality, nay, unfairness, displayed by the Russians towards the most perfect works of their own literature when they did not answer to the claims or the expectations of their party or their day. A purely aesthetic handling of the subject would not gain it full acceptance.*"

Indeed, to read the contemporary Russian onslaughts directed against Turgenev's successive masterpieces is to imagine one must be dreaming. Nearly every popular critic of the periodical press, righteous or self-righteous, is seen, tape-measure in hand, arbitrarily finding fault with Turgenev's subject, conception and treatment, disdaining or ignoring its aesthetic force, beauty and harmonious perfection. It is a crowd of critical gnats dancing airily round the great master and eagerly driving their little stings into his flesh. Even before the publication of *Smoke* (1867) Turgenev was accused of being *out of date*, and his frequent spells of residence abroad, at Baden, Paris, etc. (though he returned to Russia nearly every year), and his "life devotion" to a foreigner, Madame Viardot, helped to consolidate the story that he no longer knew the Russia of the day. And indeed there is truth in the dictum that Turgenev was pre-eminently a chronicler of the Pre-Reform days, or as he himself said, "a writer of the transition period." But the bulk of his works, even those into which no tendency could be read, such as *The Torrents of Spring* or *A Lear of the Steppes*, was never properly appreciated as aesthetic creations, so deeply imbued was the intelligent Russian with the "war-like" criticism of Drobrolubov, Tchernyshevsky, Pisarev, Mihaïlovsky, etc., critics who, in Brückner's words, "relegated aesthetics to ladies' society, and turned its critical report into a sort of pulpit for moral and social preaching." A strong reaction in Turgenev's favour was manifested at the Pushkin statue celebration in Moscow, 1879, and at his funeral obsequies in Petersburg, 1883, when two hundred and eighty-five deputations met at his grave. But, later, MM. Mihaïlovsky and Strahov, and latterly MM. Haumant, Brückner and Baring, have declared that "the general admiration" for Turgenev's genius has greatly weakened, and that Turgenev's star has paled before the stars of Tolstoy and Dostoevsky. This undercutting style of criticism—"They shadow you with Homer, knock you flat with Shakespeare," as Meredith puts it—seems a little clumsy when one reflects that not merely in vision and temperament, but in aesthetic quality, Turgenev is irreplaceable. The spiritual kingdoms of Turgenev, Tolstoy and Dostoevsky are separated as widely as are the kingdoms of Wordsworth, Byron and Shelley. It is true that for our triumphant bourgeoisies, who, bewildered, grapple with the rich profusion of facts, problems and aspects of our congested civilization, *quality* in art is little understood or prized. And Turgenev, by his art's harmonious union of form and subject, of grace and strength, of thought and emotion, in fact belongs, as Renan said, to the school of Greek perfection.

Since Turgenev is pre-eminently an intellectual force, as well as an artist with a consummate sense of beauty, it is difficult for a critic to hold the balance equitably between the social significance of Turgenev's pictures of life and the beauty of his vision. Far too little attention has been paid to him as artist. This is no doubt not merely due to the fact that while the majority of critics either naïvely ignore or take for granted his supreme quality, the more perfect is a work of art the more impossible is it to do it critical justice. The great artists, as Botticelli, who are peculiarly mannered, it is far easier to criticize and comment on than is a great artist, as Praxiteles, whose harmony of form conceals subtleties of technique unique in spiritual handling. The discussion of technical beauties, however, is not only a thankless business but tends to defeat its own object. It is better to seek to appreciate the spirit of a master, and to dwell on his human value rather than on his aesthetic originality. The present writer need scarcely add that he is dissatisfied with his inadequate discussion of Turgenev's masterpieces, but fragmentary as it is, he believes his is almost the only detailed attempt yet made in the English language.

II
YOUTH, FAMILY AND EARLY WORK

CHAPTER II

YOUTH, FAMILY AND EARLY WORK

"All my life is in my works," said Turgenev, and his biographers' account of his education and youth reveals how it was that from the age of twenty-three Turgenev was to become both an interpreter of the Russian mind to Europe and an interpreter of Western culture to his countrymen. His father, Sergey Ivanovitch, a handsome, polished officer of impoverished but ancient family, married an heiress, Varvara Petrovna Lutovinov, and their eldest son, Ivan Sergeyevitch, was born, October 28, 1818, at Orel, in central Russia. The natural loathing of the soft, poetic and impulsive boy for tyrannical harshness was accentuated by his parents', especially by his mother's, severity, unmerited whippings and punishments being his portion in the "noble and opulent country-house" at Spasskoe, where foreign tutors and governesses succeeded one another quickly. That Turgenev had before his eyes from his childhood in his capricious and despotic mother a distressing object-lesson of a typical Russian vice, viz. unbridled love of power, could only deepen his instinct for siding with weak and gentle natures. Turgenev's psychological penetration into hard, coarse and heartless characters, so antithetic to his own, seems surprising till we learn that the unscrupulous and cruel "Lutchinov," the hero of *Three Portraits*, was drawn from a maternal ancestor. From the Lutovinov family, cruel, despotic and grasping, Turgenev no doubt inherited a mental strand which enabled him to fathom the workings of hardness and cruelty in others. The injustice and humiliations he and his brothers, along with a large household of dependents, suffered at Madame Turgenev's hands,[4] early aroused in him a detestation of the system of serfdom. The touching story of *Mumu*, in which the deaf and dumb house-porter's sweetheart is forced to marry another man, while he himself is ordered to drown his pet dog by his mistress's caprice, is a true domestic chronicle. Though Madame Turgenev dearly loved her son Ivan Sergeyevitch, whose sweet and tender nature influenced her for good, her insatiable desire to domineer over others, and her violent outbursts of rage kept the household trembling before her whims. "Nobody had a right to sustain in her presence any ideas which contradicted her own," while her jealousy of her handsome husband's *affaires de cœur* embittered her days.[5] She herself had been the victim of her own upbringing, and remembered with loathing her step-father's lust and cruelty. Turgenev therefore was early inoculated with an aversion for tyrannizing in any shape or form, as well as for the prevalent forms of oppression, official or social, under Nicholas I., and as his biographers tell us, the Turgenevs were a stock noted for "a hatred of slavery and for noble and humane temperaments."[6]

[4] See "La mère d'Ivan Turguenieff," in *Tourguénieff Inconnu*, par Michel Delines.

[5] See the story *First Love*, where Turgenev describes his parents' relations.

[6] Brückner's *A Literary History of Russia*, p. 338.

A second potent influence that turned the youthful Turgenev's face definitely towards the West was his lengthy tour in Europe, 1838-41. His early education at Moscow University had been completed at the University of St. Petersburg, where his family had removed after his father's death in 1835, and where as a shy youth he saw the two great authors, Gogol and Pushkin, whose literary example was to have a profound influence on his own work. German philosophy, especially Hegel's, was at this epoch fashionable in Russia, and Turgenev, after setting out on his tour with his mother's blessing, attended by a valet, arrived in Berlin, where he drank deep of Goethe's, Schiller's and Heine's works, and where his ardent discussions with his circle of students on life, art, politics and metaphysics crystallized his aspirations for European culture. A tour on the Rhine, in Switzerland and in Italy effectually widened his outlook, and he returned to Spasskoe in 1841, bringing with him his narrative poem "Parasha."

Undoubtedly conflicting influences, such as Byron, Pushkin and Lermontov, are visible in Turgenev's youthful, romantic poems, "Parasha," and various others (1837-47), which we shall not discuss here, or his half-dozen plays (1845-52), which last, however excellent, did not give his genius sufficient scope.[7] Much ingenuity has been exercised, especially by French critics,[8] in ascribing Turgenev's literary debts to authors as diverse as Maria Edgeworth, Victor Hugo, Balzac, Schiller, Goethe, Heine, Auerbach, Dal, Grigorovitch, Dickens, etc. But it would be a waste of time to analyse Turgenev's work for traces of contemporary authors, though George Sand's stories of French peasant life had undoubtedly deeply influenced him. With Pushkin as classical model for clarity of style, and with Gogol as his model for direct painting from everyday life, Turgenev belongs to "the natural school" of the 'forties, the school of the realists championed by the critic Byelinsky, then all-powerful with the rising men. It is true that a vein of romanticism crops up here and there in various of Turgenev's tales, and that a definite strain of lyrical sentimentalism in occasional passages may be credited to German influence. But in almost his first story, *The Duellist* (1846), we find a complete break with the traditions of the romantic school, traditions which are indeed here turned inside out.[9] Here it is evident that a new master is in the field, "a painter of realities" as Byelinsky soon declared.[10] The story is of much significance, as exemplifying Turgenev's clear-eyed, deep apprehension of character, and his creative penetration through *beauty of feeling*. It is to be noted how the coarse bullying insolence of the officer, Lutchkov (who out of envious spleen kills in a duel his friend, the refined and generous Kister), is betrayed *by the absence of any tender or chivalrous emotion for women.* Filled with his own male self-complacency, and contemptuous of women, Lutchkov comes to his interview with the fresh, innocent girl Masha, whom he alarms by his coarse swagger. To cover his brutal egoistic feeling he roughly kisses the shrinking girl, but she shudders and darts away. "What are you afraid of? Come, stop that.... That's all nonsense," he says hoarsely, as he approaches her, terribly confused, with a disagreeable smile on his twisted lips, while patches of red came out on his face.

[7] "Parasha" was warmly praised by Byelinsky in 1843, in an article in *Annals of the Fatherland*. Of the six Plays, which were revived from time to time, *The Bachelor* (1849) is perhaps the strongest. In later years Turgenev disclaimed any interest in his dramas, and declared that towards his poems he felt an antipathy almost physical.

[8] Haumant, Delines, Waliszewski, etc.

[9] M. Haumant has been at great pains to show that Turgenev in his early prose and verse "commenced by appropriating the form and the subjects of the romantics of the 'twenties and the 'thirties, that his 'half revolt' against the romantic convention became accentuated later, and that we find in the plays and poems a 'degradation of the romantic heroes' of Pushkin and Lermontov" (Haumant, pp. 113-122). Although there is not a little truth in his thesis, M. Haumant has forgotten to add that the *social atmosphere* of the preceding generation, as well as of its literature, music and art, was "romantic," and that the youth of the period, as well as the heroes of Goethe and Stendhal, did act, think and feel in a "romantic" manner.

[10] Byelinsky, in his criticism on *Hor and Kalinitch*, says: "His talent is not suited to true lyrics. He can only paint from real life what he has seen or *studied*. He can create, but only with the materials given by nature. It is not a copy of the real; nature has not given the author innate ideas, but he has to find them; the author transforms the real, following his artistic ideal, and so his picture becomes more living. He knows how to render faithfully a character or a fact he has observed.... Nature has given Turgenev this capacity of observing, of understanding, and of appreciating faithfully and quickly each fact, of divining its cause and consequences, and, when facts are lacking, of supplying the factors by just divination."

Could anything describe better the brutal spirit of the man who, out of spiteful envy, to revenge his slighted self-love, kills his own friend, Kister, in a duel? Turgenev's description of Kister must be remarked, for the latter in his "good nature, modesty, warm-heartedness and *natural inclination for everything beautiful*" is the twin-soul of his creator. Turgenev's lifelong readiness to lose sight of himself in appreciation of others, even of the men who abused his good offices and repaid him with ingratitude, was notorious.[11] One may assert that Turgenev's character was thus early expressed in four dominant traits, viz. a generous tenderness of heart, an enthusiasm for the good, sensitiveness to beauty of form and feeling, an infinite capacity for the passion of love. These qualities are manifest in his first work of importance, *A Sportsman's Sketches* (1847-51), an epoch-making book which profoundly affected Russian society and had no small influence in hastening the Emancipation of the Serfs in 1861-63.

[11] For example, Turgenev warmly commended Dostoevsky's works to foreign critics, after the latter had perpetrated the spiteful libel on him in *The Possessed*.

III
"A SPORTSMAN'S SKETCHES"

CHAPTER III

"A SPORTSMAN'S SKETCHES"—"NATURE AND MAN"—THE SECRET OF TURGENEV'S ART

At this date, 1847, Russia, long prostrate beneath the drill sergeants of that "paternal" autocrat Nicholas I.,[12] with the lynx-eyed police rule, servile press and general atmosphere of bureaucratic subservience stupefying the country, was slowly awakening to the new ideas of reform. Grigorovitch's novel *The Village* (1846), which painted the wretched life of the serfs, marked the changing current of social ideas, but to Turgenev was to fall the honour of hastening "the Emancipation." There is perhaps a little exaggeration in this eloquent passage of M. de Vogüé: "Russia saw its own image with alarm in the mirror of serfdom held towards it. A shiver passed through the land: in a day Turgenev became famous, and his cause was half won.... I have said that serfdom stood condemned in everybody's heart, even in the Emperor Nicholas's." But we are assured by Turgenev himself that Alexander II.'s resolution to abolish serfdom was due in no small part to *A Sportsman's Sketches*. The old generation in fact was soon to pass away with Nicholas's rule. As the sketch "The Peasant Proprietor Ovsyanikov" demonstrates, to this old race of landowners, frankly despotic in their manners, was succeeding a milder class—one which "did not like the old methods," but was ineffective and self-distrustful. And it was to this younger Russia in silent protest against the "official nationalism" prescribed by the ministers of Nicholas, and against the stagnation of provincial life which Gogol had satirized so unsparingly in *Dead Souls* (1842), that Turgenev made his appeal with his first sketch "Hor and Kalinitch" in the magazine *The Contemporary*. Turgenev's reputation was made, and Byelinsky, who declared that Turgenev was "not a creator but a painter of realities," immediately predicted his future greatness. The other, *A Sportsman's Sketches*, as they appeared, one by one, were eagerly seized on by the public, who felt that this new talent was revealing deep-welling springs of individuality in the Russian nature, hitherto unrecorded.

[12] "The teaching of philosophy was proscribed in all the schools, and in all the universities of the Empire; admission to which had now been reduced in numbers. The classics were similarly ostracised. Historical publications were put under a censor's control, which was tantamount to a prohibition. No history of modern times, *i.e.* of the seventeenth or eighteenth centuries, was allowed to be taught in any form whatsoever."—E. M. DE VOGÜÉ.

Though Russian society was profoundly moved by Turgenev's picture of serfdom, it was in truth the triumph of the pure artist, of the writer who saw man's fugitive life in relation to the vast, universal drama of nature, that made

A Sportsman's Sketches acceptable to all. One may compare the book's atmosphere to some woodland's tender morning air quivering with light, which transmits the ringing voices of men in all their meaning inflections. The voices rise, in joy or strife or passion, then die away in silence, and we hear the gentle stir and murmur of the leaves as the wind passes, while afar swells the roar of the deep forest. Turgenev's spiritual vision resembles this silvery light and air which register equally the most exquisite vibration of human aspiration and the dissonance of men's folly and misery. The sweet and tender depths of the author's spirit served, so to say, as a sensitive mirror which reflected impassively the struggle between the forces of worldly craft and the appeal of all humble, neglected and suffering creatures. "The Tryst" is an example of the artist's exquisite responsiveness both to the fleeting moods of nature and the conflicts of human feeling. Thus the sufferings of the young peasant girl, poor Akoulina, at the hands of her conceited lover, the pampered valet, Viktor, are so blended with the woodland scene and our last view of "the empty cart rattling over the bare hillside, the low sinking sun in the pale clear sky, the gusty wind scudding over the stubble fields, the bright but chill smile of fading nature," that one can scarcely dissociate the girl's distress from the landscape. An illusion! but one that great literature—for example, the *Odyssey*—fosters. When we look over the face of a wide-stretching landscape each tiny hamlet and its dwellers appear to the eye as a little point of human activity, and each environment, again, as the outcome of an endless chain of forces, seen and unseen in nature. Man, earth and heaven—it is the trinity always suggested in the work of the great poets.

But the vast background of nature need not be always before the eyes of an audience. In "The Hamlet of the Shtchigri District," for instance, where—through the railings of an embittered man against the petty boredom of provincial life, together with a characteristically Russian confession of his own sloth and mediocrity—we breathe the heated air of a big landowner's house, the window on nature is, so to say, shut down. So in "Lebedyan" the bustle and humours of a horse-fair in the streets of a small country town, and in "The Country House" the sordid manoeuvres of the stewards and clerks of the lazy landed proprietor, Madame Losnyakov, against their victims, the peasants on the estate, exclude the fresh atmosphere of forest and steppe. But even so we are conscious that the sky and earth encompass these people's meetings in market-place and inns, in posting-stations, peasants' huts and landowners' domains, and always a faint undertone murmurs to us that each generation is like a wave passing in the immensity of sea. Sometimes, as in "The District Doctor," a tragedy within four walls is shut in by a feeling of sudden night and the isolation of the wintry fields. Sometimes, as in "Biryuk," the outbreak of a despairing peasant is reflected in the fleeting storm-clouds and lashing rain of a storm in the forest. But the people's figures are always seen *in just relation to their surroundings, to their fellows and to nature.*

By the relations of a man with his neighbours and their ideas, a man's character is focussed for us and his place in his environment determined. Thus in "Raspberry Spring" the old steward Tuman's complacent panegyrics on the lavish ways of his former master, a grand seigneur of Catherine's time, are a meaning accompaniment to the misery of Vlass the harassed serf. Vlass has just returned from his sad errand to Moscow (his son has died there penniless), where he has had his master's door shut in his face, and he has been ordered to return and pay the bailiff his arrears of rent. Whether under the ancient régime of Catherine, or of Nicholas I., Vlass is the "poor man" of Scripture whose face is ground by the rich. All the irony of poor Vlass's existence steals upon us while we hear the old steward's voice descanting on the dead count's sumptuous banquets, on his cooks and fiddlers and the low-born mistresses who brought him to ruin; while the humble peasant sits still and hears, too, of the "embroidered coats, wigs, canes, perfumes, *eau de cologne*, snuff-boxes, of the huge pictures ordered from Paris!" It is the cruelty, passive or active, innate in the web of human existence that murmurs here in the bass.

The parts in just relation to the whole scheme of existence, that is the secret of Turgenev's supremacy, and what a piercing instinct for the relative values of men's motives and actions is revealed by his calm, clear scrutiny! Observe in "The Agent" how the old serf Antip's weeping protest against his family's ruin at the hands of the tyrannous agent Sofron is made in *the model village* Shiplova, with its tidy farm-buildings and new windmill and threshing-floors, its rich stacks and hemp-fields "all in excellent order." It is Sofron, the man of "first rate administrative power," so honey-tongued before the gentry, who farms four hundred acres of his own, and trades in horses and stock and corn and hemp, it is this petty despot in his prosperity who "is harrying the peasants out of their lives." "He is sharp, awfully sharp, and rich, too, the beast!" says the Ryabovo peasant. Behind the tyrannous bailiff Sofron is the owner of Shiplova, the polished Mr. Pyenotchkin, a retired officer of the Guards, who has mixed in the highest society. Mr. Pyenotchkin is a man *comme il faut*, but when he finds that his luckless footman has forgotten to warm the wine, he simply raises his eyebrows and orders his major-domo to "make the necessary arrangements"—to have Fyodor flogged! Here is progress on Western lines comfortably cheek by jowl with serfdom! Of course the sting, here, for the Russian conscience lay precisely in this juxtaposition of old and new, and in the knowledge that the most progressive landowner could exercise his legal right to sell his peasants, send a man away as a conscript, and separate him from his family. But it is well to note that only three or four of the *Sportsman's Sketches* expose typical cases of a landlord's tyranny and the anachronism of this mediaeval survival—serfdom.

One of these cases is "Yermolai and the Miller's Wife," a sketch which for the calm breadth of vision in its exposure of serfdom is flawless. In "Yermolai" note how Turgenev by a series of discreet intermittent touches brings his people on the scene, and how the tranquil description of the winding river, the Ista, with its stony banks and cold clear streams and rugged precipitous banks, prepares us for the story of poor Arina's sorrows and of the self-complacent master's tyranny. Because Madame Zvyerkoff makes it a rule never to keep married lady's maids, poor Arina is disgraced, her lover sent away as a soldier, and she herself is married to the miller, who has offered a price for her. This distressing episode, though the central theme, is introduced subtly by a side wind after we have accompanied the narrator and the tall gaunt huntsman, Yermolai, to the Ista's banks, where the two sportsmen are benighted and seek sleep in the outhouse of a mill. The bull-necked, fat-bellied miller sends out his wife with a message to them, and this woman with her refined, mournful eyes is none other than the unfortunate Arina, with whom Yermolai is on old, familiar terms. The sportsman-narrator, who has been dozing in the hay, wakes and soon gathers from the snatches of talk between the pair the details of Arina's listless melancholy days after her child's death. Her bitter situation is flashed upon us in Yermolai's suggestion that she shall pay a visit to him in his hut when his own wife is away from home! She changes the subject and soon walks away, and Yermolai's peasant callousness is indicated in his yawning answer to his master's questions. Then this story of a woman's sorrow is brought to a close by one of those exquisite nature touches which brings us back again to the infinite life of the encompassing earth and sky:

"'And do you know her lover, Petrushka?'

"'Piotr Vassilyevitch? Of course I know him.'

"'Where is he now?'

"'He was sent for a soldier.'

"We were silent for a while.

"'She doesn't seem very well?' I asked Yermolai at last.

"'I should think not! To-morrow, I say, we shall have good sport. A little sleep now would do us no harm.'

"A flock of wild ducks swept whizzing over our heads, and we heard them drop down into the river not far from us. It was quite dark, and it began to be cold; in the thicket sounded the melodious notes of a nightingale. We buried ourselves in the hay and fell asleep!"

By the descriptions of the landscape in "Yermolai and the Miller's Wife" Turgenev subtly introduces the sense into our minds of nature's vastness, of her infinity, of which the spectacle of man's social injustice and distress becomes indissolubly part. Here there is nothing of the reformer's *parti-pris* in the picture. Turgenev's fluid, sympathetic perceptions blend into a flow of creative mood, in which the relations of men to their surroundings, and the significance of their actions, their feelings, their fate are seen as parts of the universal, dominating scheme of things. And this flow of mood in Turgenev is his creative secret: as when music flows from a distance to the listener over the darkening fields immediately the rough coarse earth, with all its grinding, petty monotony melts into harmony, and life is seen in its mysterious immensity, not merely in its puzzling discrepancy of gaps, and contradictions and confusions. Turgenev's work, at its best, gives us the sense of looking beyond the heads of the moving human figures, out to the infinite horizon.

Although in Turgenev's pellucid art each touch seems simple, the whole effect is highly complex, depending upon an infinite variety of shades of tone. Let us finish by examining his complex method in "The Singers." In the first twenty lines the author etches the cheerless aspect of "the unlucky hamlet of Kolotovka, which lies on the slope of a barren hill … yet all the surrounding inhabitants know the road to Kolotovka well; they go there often and are always glad to go." It is not merely the tavern "The Welcome Resort," but the tavern-keeper Nikolai Ivanitch that attracts them, for his shrewd alertness and geniality are an influence far and wide in the neighbourhood. Turgenev now introduces his main theme by a variation *in tempo*. He describes how the narrator on a blazing hot July day is slowly dragging his feet up the Kolotovka ravine towards the Inn, when he overhears one man calling to another to come and hear a singing competition between Yashka the Turk and the booth-keeper from Zhizdry. The narrator's curiosity is stirred, and he follows the villagers into the bar-room, where he finds the assembled company, who are urging the two singers to begin. The men toss and the lot falls on the booth-keeper. Having riveted our attention, Turgenev now increases his hold on us by sketching the life and character of three village characters, "the Gabbler," "the Blinkard" and "the Wild Master." We examine the village audience till the booth-keeper at last steps forward and sings. For a time the booth-keeper does not evoke the enthusiasm of the critical villagers, but at last they are conquered by his bold flourishes and daring trills, and they shout their applause. The booth-keeper's song is the triumph of technique and of training, and he carries away his hearers, while "the Gabbler" bawls: "You've won, brother, you've won!" But "the Wild Master" silences "the Gabbler" with an oath and calls on Yashka to begin. And now follows an entrancing description of the power of genius to sway the heart:

"'Come, that's enough; don't be timid. For shame! ... why go back?... Sing the best you can, by God's gift.'

"And the Wild Master looked down expectant. Yakov was silent for a minute; he glanced round, and covered his face with his hand. All had their eyes simply fastened upon him, especially the booth-keeper, on whose face a faint, involuntary uneasiness could be seen through his habitual expression of self-confidence and the triumph of his success. He leant back against the wall, and again put both hands under him, but did not swing his legs as before. When at last Yakov uncovered his face it was pale as a dead man's; his eyes gleamed faintly under their drooping lashes. He gave a deep sigh, and began to sing.... The first sound of his voice was faint and unequal, and seemed not to come from his chest, but to be wafted from somewhere afar off, as though it had floated by chance into the room. A strange effect was produced on all of us by this trembling, resonant note; we glanced at one another, and Nikolai Ivanitch's wife seemed to draw herself up. This first note was followed by another, bolder and prolonged, but still obviously quivering, like a harp-string when suddenly struck by a stray finger it throbs in a last, swiftly-dying tremble; the second was followed by a third, and, gradually gaining fire and breadth, the strains swelled into a pathetic melody. 'Not one little path ran into the field,' he sang, and sweet and mournful it was in our ears. I have seldom, I must confess, heard a voice like it; it was slightly hoarse, and not perfectly true; there was even something morbid about it at first; but it had genuine depth of passion, and youth and sweetness, and a sort of fascinating careless, pathetic melancholy. A spirit of truth and fire, a Russian spirit, was sounding and breathing in that voice, and it seemed to go straight to your heart, to go straight to all that was Russian in it. The song swelled and flowed. Yakov was clearly carried away by enthusiasm; he was not timid now; he surrendered himself wholly to the rapture of his art; his voice no longer trembled; it quivered; but with a scarce perceptible inward quiver of passion, which pierces like an arrow to the very soul of the listeners, and he steadily gained strength and firmness and breadth. I remember I once saw at sunset on a flat sandy shore, when the tide was low and the sea's roar came weighty and menacing from the distance, a great white sea-gull; it sat motionless, its silky bosom facing the crimson glow of the setting sun, and only now and then opening wide its great wings to greet the well-known sea, to greet the sinking lurid sun: I recalled it, as I heard Yakov. He sang, utterly forgetful of his rival and all of us; he seemed supported, as a bold swimmer by the waves, by our silent, passionate sympathy. He sang, and in every sound of his voice one seemed to feel something dear and akin to us, something of breadth and space, as though the familiar steppes were unfolding before our eyes and stretching away into endless distance. I felt the tears gathering in my bosom and rising to my eyes; suddenly I was struck by dull, smothered sobs.... I looked round— the innkeeper's wife was weeping, her bosom pressed close to the window. Yakov threw a quick glance at her, and he sang more sweetly, more melodiously than ever; Nikolai Ivanitch looked down; the Blinkard turned away; the Gabbler, quite touched, stood, his gaping mouth stupidly open; the humble peasant was sobbing softly in the corner and shaking his head with a plaintive murmur; and on the iron visage of the Wild Master, from under his overhanging brows there slowly rolled a heavy tear; the booth-keeper raised his clenched fists to his brow, and did not stir.... I don't know how the general emotion would have ended if Yakov had not suddenly come to a full stop on a high, exceptionally shrill note, as though his voice had broken. No one called out or even stirred; every one seemed to be waiting to see whether he was not going to sing more; but he opened his eyes as though wondering at our silence, looked round at all of us with a face of enquiry, and saw that the victory was his....

"'Yasha,' said the Wild Master, laying his hand on his shoulder, and he could say no more.

"We stood, as it were, petrified. The booth-keeper softly rose and went up to Yakov.

"'You ... yours ... you've won,' he articulated at last with an effort, and rushed out of the room."

An artist less consummate than Turgenev would have ended here. But the sequel immeasurably heightens the whole effect by plunging us into the mournful, ever-running springs of human tragedy—the eclipse of man's spiritual instincts by the emergence of his underlying animalism. Observe there is not a trace of ethical feeling in the mournful close. It is simply the way of life:

"... When I waked up, everything was in darkness; the hay scattered around smelt strong, and was slightly damp; through the slender rafters of the half-open roof pale stars were faintly twinkling. I went out. The glow of sunset had long died away, and its last trace showed in a faint light on the horizon; but above the freshness of the night there was still a feeling of heat in the atmosphere, lately baked through by the sun, and the breast still craved for a draught of cool air. There was no wind nor were there any clouds; the sky all round was clear and transparently dark, softly glimmering with innumerable, but scarcely visible stars. There were lights twinkling about the village; from the flaring tavern close by rose a confused, discordant din, amid which I fancied I recognized the voice of Yakov. Violent laughter came from there in an outburst at times. I went up to the little window and pressed my face against the pane. I saw a cheerless, though varied and animated scene; all were drunk—all from Yakov upwards. With breast bared, he sat on a bench, and singing in a thick voice a street song to a dance tune, he lazily fingered and strummed on the strings of a guitar. His moist hair hung in tufts over his fearfully pale face. In the middle of the room, the Gabbler, completely 'screwed,' and without his coat, was hopping about in a dance before the peasant in the grey smock; the peasant, on his side, was with difficulty stamping and scraping with his feet, and grinning meaninglessly over his dishevelled beard; he waved one hand from time to time, as much as to say, 'Here goes!' Nothing could be more ludicrous than his face; however much he twitched up his eyebrows, his heavy lids would hardly rise, but seemed lying upon his scarcely-visible, dim, and mawkish eyes. He was in that amiable frame of mind of a perfectly intoxicated man, when every passer-by, directly he looks him in the face, is sure to say, 'Bless you, brother, bless you!' The Blinkard, as red as a lobster, and his nostrils dilated wide, was laughing malignantly in a corner; only Nikolai Ivanitch, as befits a good tavern-keeper, preserved his composure unchanged. The room was thronged with many new faces, but the Wild Master I did not see in it.

"I turned away with rapid steps and began descending the hill on which Kolotovka lies. At the foot of this hill stretches a wide plain; plunged in the misty waves of the evening haze, it seemed more immense, and was, as it were, merged in the darkening sky. I marched with long strides along the road by the ravine, when all at once, from somewhere far away in the plain, came a boy's clear voice: 'Antropka! Antropka-a-a...!' He shouted in obstinate and tearful desperation, with long, long drawing out of the last syllable.

"He was silent for a few instants, and started shouting again. His voice rang out clear in the still, lightly slumbering air. Thirty times at least he had called the name, Antropka. When suddenly, from the farthest end of the plain, as though from another world, there floated a scarcely audible reply:

"'Wha-a-t?'

"The boy's voice shouted back at once with gleeful exasperation:

"'Come here, devil! woo-od imp!'

"'What fo-or?' replied the other, after a long interval.

"'Because dad wants to thrash you!' the first voice shouted back hurriedly.

"The second voice did not call back again, and the boy fell to shouting 'Antropka' once more. His cries, fainter and less and less frequent, still floated up to my ears, when it had grown completely dark, and I had turned the corner of the wood that skirts my village and lies over three miles from Kolotovka ... 'Antropka-a-a!' was still audible in the air, filled with the shadows of the night."

In the above passage the feeling of the shadowy earth, the mist, the great plain and the floating cries rarefies the village atmosphere of human commonness. By such a representation of the people's figures, seen in just relation to their surroundings, to their fellows, and to nature, Turgenev's art secures for his picture poetic harmony, and renders these finer cadences in the turmoil of life which ears less sensitive than his fail to hear! *The parts in just relation to the whole scheme of human existence.* Man, earth and heaven—it is the secret of the perfection of the great poets.

IV
"RUDIN"

CHAPTER IV

"RUDIN"

The biographers tell us that Turgenev left Russia again in 1847, for the sake of being near Pauline Garcia, the famous singer (afterwards Madame Viardot), whom he adored all his life; that he left her in Berlin, visited Salzbrunn with the critic Byelinsky, who was dying of consumption, and then proceeded to Paris, Brussels, Lyons and Courtavenel. In Paris he works incessantly, producing plays and short stories and most of the series of *A Sportsman's Sketches*; makes friends with Hertzen and George Sand; studies the French classics and avows his democratic sympathies, without any illusions as to the good-for-nothingness of "the Reds." In the autumn of 1858 he returns to Russia, recalled by news of the grave illness of his mother, who, however, refused to be reconciled with her two sons, whom she tried to disinherit on her deathbed. Turgenev was henceforward a rich man. In 1852 *A Sportsman's Sketches* appeared in book form, and in April of the same year, for writing a sympathetic article on Gogol's death, Turgenev was ordered a month's detention in a police-station and then confined to his estate at Spasskoe.[13]

[13] "I am confined in a police-station by the Emperor's orders for having printed a short article on Gogol in a Moscow journal. This was only a pretext, the article itself being perfectly insignificant. They have looked at me askance for a long time, and they have laid hold of this pretext at the first opportunity. I do not complain of the Emperor; the matter has been so deceitfully represented to him that he couldn't have acted otherwise. They have wished to put a stop on all that is being said on Gogol's death, and they have not been sorry, at the same time, to place an embargo on my literary activity."— Letter to M. and Mme. Viardot, May 13, 1852.

Turgenev notes that his imperious desire to escape to Europe indicated "Possibly something lacking in my character or force of will." But he declares, "I should never have written *A Sportsman's Sketches* had I remained in Russia.... It was impossible for me to remain and breathe the same air that gave life to everything I abhorred." The persecution of his literary forerunners and contemporaries by the Autocracy was continuous. Pushkin's humiliation and subjection to official authority; Lermontov's exile to the Caucasus; Tchaadaev declared insane by bureaucratic order and confined to a mad-house; Gogol's recantation of *Dead Souls* and relapse into feeble mysticism; Hertzen's expatriation; Dostoevsky's and Petrashevsky's exile to the mines of Siberia; Saltykov's banishment, etc., the list of the intellectual and creative minds gagged or stifled under Nicholas I. is endless. And Turgenev's mild and generous spirit was designed neither for political partisanship nor for active revolt. He has indeed been accused of timidity,[14] and cowardice by uncompromising Radicals and Revolutionaries. But his life-work is the answer to these ill-considered allegations. Spiritual enfranchisement was impossible in "the swamp of Petersburg with its Winter Palace, eight Ministries, three Polices, the most Holy Synod, and all the exalted family with their German relatives," as Hertzen wittily put it later; and by faring abroad and by inhaling deep draughts of free European air Turgenev was enabled, in his own phrase, "to strike the enemy from a distance."

[14] In an access of self-reproach he once declared to a friend that his character was comprised in one word—"poltroon."

His exile for a year and a half to his own estate was, however, by no means a bad thing for his own self-development. Years afterwards he wrote: "All was for the best.... My being under arrest and in the country proved to my undeniable advantage; it brought me close to those sides of Russian life which, in the ordinary course of things, would probably have escaped my observation." He consoled himself with shooting, with music, with reading, with literary composition, and it is to this enforced detention in Russia that, no doubt, we owe the masterpiece *Rudin* (1855), which he rewrote many times, declaring to Aksakov that none of his other stories had ever given him so much trouble. In fact this novel, in grace, ease and strength, has the quality of finished statuary.

Though sixty years have passed since the appearance of *Rudin*, no dust has gathered on the novel, so original is the leading figure. The portrait of the hero who typifies the failure of the Russian *intelligentsia* of the "forties' to do more than talk, is as arresting as the day on which it was painted. In him Turgenev creates a fresh variety of idealist, the orator sapped by the love of his own words. Rudin is Russian in the combination of his soft, wavering will, his lofty enthusiasm for ideas, and his rather naïve sincerity: in other respects, he might be a western European. Behind him we feel generations of easygoing manorial gentlefolk regarding in surprise this curious descendant, whose clever brain is aglow with a passion for "eternal truth" and for the "general principles" of German philosophy. One is haunted by a sense of Rudin's cousinship to other famous idealists in life and literature; he shows affinities both to a contemporary, Coleridge, and to a famous successor, Ibsen's *Brand*.

English idealism in general is both a covering for mundane interests, and a spiritual compromise with those same interests. An English Rudin would have gone into the Church, and as a Canon or Bishop would have attained celebrity by his gift of lofty and magnetic eloquence. But a Russian Rudin does not succeed in buttering his bread; it is both his unworldliness and lack of will that bring his powers to nought. Rudin can and does indeed, deceive himself; but the strands of hypocrisy in his nature are too fragmentary to bring him worldly success.

Of Turgenev's six novels, *Rudin* is the most perfect in form, by the harmony of its parts and absolute grace of modelling.[15] Everywhere the master's chisel has fined away his material to attain the most delicately firm contours. The grouping of the character is a lesson in harmonious arrangement. Note by what simple, natural steps one passes from the outer circle of the neighbours of the wealthy patroness of art and letters, Darya Mihailovna, to the inner circle of her household. The cold, suave egoism of the lady of the manor is admirably set off by the sketches of her dependents, the simple young tutor, Bassistoff, her young Jewish *protégé* Pandalevsky, and the cynic Pigasov. The household is expecting the arrival of a guest, a Baron Muffel, but in his place arrives his acquaintance, Dmitri Rudin, slightly shabby, but of pre-possessing address.

[15] For a discussion of Turgenev's debt to George Sand's novel, *Horace*, see M. Halperine-Kaminsky's *Tourguéneff and his French Circle*, p. 301.

A master of eloquent language, Rudin conquers his hearers by his fine bearing and brilliant talk. But notice that the effect he instantaneously produces holds in germ all the after development of the story. Volintsev fears in him a rival for Natalya's love; Pandalevsky is on his guard against the clever stranger who may dispossess him in the favour of the mistress of the house; Natalya falls in love with the newcomer who has fired her girlish imagination; while her mother, Darya Mihailovna, is planning to keep Rudin, this coming lion, in her house to adorn her salon. The structure of the story, beautifully planned, is a lesson in the directness and ease of artistic development. Everything flows, simply and inevitably, from the actions of the group of characters, quickened and watchful after Rudin's arrival.

As an example of Turgenev's skill in drawing a man with a dozen touches, and of exposing the mainspring of his nature by a few of his words and actions, consider the Jewish-looking youth, Pandalevsky; with the slight, exact strokes of his chisel Turgenev here graves a perfect intaglio. Pandalevsky, in the opening pages, meeting the charming Alexandra Pavlovna on her walk, offers her his arm, *unasked*. "She took it." After some flowery remarks, Pandalevsky, presuming further, says, "Allow me to offer you this lovely wild flower." Alexandra Pavlovna did not refuse it, but "after a few steps, let it drop on the path." The sensitive woman is repelled by the young Jew's familiarity and his thickness of skin, and indeed Pandalevsky has scarcely turned his back on her, when he transfers his interest to a peasant girl working in the field, and so coarse is his talk that she stops her ears and mutters, "Go away, sir; upon my word!"

Again, note how the characters all reveal themselves by their unconscious behaviour. On the night of Rudin's unexpected arrival, while Bassistoff sits up, pouring out his soul in an eloquent letter to a friend, and Natalya cannot sleep for thinking of Rudin's glowing eloquence, "Pandalevsky went to bed, and as he took off his daintily embroidered braces, he said aloud, 'A very smart fellow,' and suddenly, looking harshly at his page, ordered him out of the room." By this little revelation of his mean spirit the young Jew prepares us for his furtive suspicion of Rudin, and for his playing the spy subsequently. By a word, a gesture, a look, psychologically exact, Turgenev secures thus in a sentence effects which it takes his rivals a paragraph or a page to make clear to us. Thus his scenes always appeal by their aesthetic ease and grace.

Remark again how swift, precise and final is Turgenev's exploration of Rudin's character. Tired of wandering, Rudin, as Darya Mihailovna's guest, is glad to have found a congenial circle, perhaps indeed a home, but while every one seems to listen eagerly to him, and he lays down the law to the household, a cold undercurrent of criticism is already felt threatening his position. One of the neighbours, Lezhnyov, had been at college with Rudin in youth, and from his talk about their past relations one learns why Rudin, despite his genius, has not succeeded in life. He is a theorist and he has never really understood human nature. So much so is this indeed that Rudin does not realize in time that Natalya, this girl "of an ardent, true and passionate nature," has fallen in love with him, and exalts him as her spiritual teacher. And when Rudin's eyes are opened this fatal flaw in his character is seen. He lives only for his ideas and for his audience; his great, his sole power lies in the magic of his stimulating, flowing oratory. He is a master of words, but he cannot act. Lezhnyov is right in declaring that Rudin in his relations with others, even in his love affairs, "only needs a fresh opportunity of speechifying and giving vent to his fine talk, and that's what he can't live without." Rudin, carried away by the discovery of Natalya's love, pretends and simulates love for her, but his "passion" is shown to be hollow when the young girl comes to warn him that Pandalevsky, spying on them, has betrayed their secret meetings to her mother, who is angry and jealous that Rudin should be paying court to her daughter. Rudin is in consternation at the news. He has been so intent on his eloquent feelings that he has not faced the practical difficulties. And he has made no plans to face the future. But let us quote the scene:

> "'And what advice can I give you, Natalya Alexyevna?'
>
> "'What advice? You are a man; I am used to trusting to you. I shall trust you to the end. Tell me, what are your plans?'

"'My plans.... Your mother will certainly turn me out of the house.'

"'Perhaps.... She told me yesterday that I must break off all acquaintance with you.... But you do not answer my question?'

"'What question?'

"'What do you think we must do now?'

"'What we must do?' replied Rudin; 'of course submit.'

"'Submit,' repeated Natalya slowly, and her lips turned white.

"'Submit to destiny,' continued Rudin. 'What is to be done?... I know very well how bitter it is, how painful, how unendurable. But consider yourself, Natalya Alexyevna; I am poor. It is true I could work; but even if I were a rich man, could you bear a violent separation from your family, your mother's anger?... No, Natalya Alexyevna; it is useless even to think of it. It is clear it was not fated for us to live together, and the happiness of which I dreamed is not for me!'

"All at once Natalya hid her face in her hands and began to weep. Rudin went up to her.

"'Natalya Alexyevna! Dear Natalya!' he said with warmth, 'do not cry, for God's sake do not torture me, be comforted.'

"Natalya raised her head.

"'You tell me to be comforted!' she began, and her eyes blazed through her tears; 'I am not weeping for what you suppose—I am not sad for that; I am sad because I have been deceived in you.... What! I come to you for counsel, and at such a moment!—and your first word is submit! submit! So this is how you translate your talk of independence, of sacrifice which....'

"Her voice broke down.

"'But, Natalya Alexyevna,' began Rudin in confusion, 'remember—I do not disown my words—only——'

"'You asked me,' she continued with new force, 'what I answered my mother, when she declared she would sooner

> agree to my death than my marriage to you; I answered that I would sooner die than marry any other man.... And you say, "Submit!" It must be that she is right; you must, through having nothing to do, through being bored, have been playing with me.'
>
> "'I swear to you, Natalya Alexyevna—I assure you,' maintained Rudin.
>
> "But she did not listen to him."

Natalya's passionate answer: "I told my mother that I would die sooner than marry any other man.... And you say 'submit'!" passes through Rudin's self-esteem like a knife. He protests vainly again and again his love. But he has exposed his ambiguous emptiness too fully. And now he must leave Darya Mihailovna's household, discredited in his own, in Natalya's and in everybody's eyes.

Remark in the passage quoted above how the conflicting currents of the girl's passionate warmth and the man's ambiguous reasoning—like hot and cold springs mingling—flow in a form beautiful by its grace of line. The scene is graven as lightly, yet as durably as an antique Greek gem. One must emphasize this union of soft warmth and grace in Turgenev's work, for it is one of his special characteristics. While the beauty of his feeling declares itself by its purity of tone, all the mental shades of a scene or a conversation are unfolded with flowing, flexible grace. Even a piece of mental analysis, a synthesis of the internal life of character, and of pure thought, are stamped with the spontaneous gestures of life. And calm and mellow tenderness seems to emanate, as a secret essence, from his pictures. We cite a little passage, famous in Russian literature, where Turgenev sketches a portrait of Byelinsky, under the pseudonym of Pokorsky, Rudin's friend:

> "'... He took pity on me, perhaps; anyway, he took me by the arm and led me away to his lodging.'
>
> "'Was that Rudin?' asked Alexandra Pavlovna.
>
> "'No, it was not Rudin ... it was a man ... he is dead now ... he was an extraordinary man. His name was Pokorsky. To describe him in a few words is beyond my powers, but directly one begins to speak of him, one does not want to speak of any one else. He had a noble, pure heart, and an intelligence such as I have never met since. Pokorsky lived in a little, low-pitched room, in an attic of an old wooden house. He was very poor, and supported himself somehow by giving lessons. Sometimes he had not even a cup of tea to offer to his friends, and his only sofa was so shaky that it

was like being on board ship. But in spite of these discomforts a great many people used to go and see him. Every one loved him; he drew all hearts to him. You would not believe what sweetness and happiness there was in sitting in his poor little room! It was in his room I met Rudin. He had already parted from his prince before then.'

"'What was there so exceptional in this Pokorsky?' asked Alexandra Pavlovna.

"'How can I tell you? Poetry and truth—that was what drew us all to him. For all his clear, broad intellect he was as sweet and simple as a child.... Pokorsky and Rudin were very unlike. There was more flash and brilliance about Rudin, more fluency, and perhaps more enthusiasm. He appeared far more gifted than Pokorsky, and yet all the while he was a poor creature by comparison. Rudin was excellent at developing any idea, he was capital in argument, but his ideas did not come from his own brain; he borrowed them from others, especially from Pokorsky: Pokorsky was quiet and soft—even weak in appearance—and he was fond of women to distraction, and fond of dissipation, and he would never take an insult from any one. Rudin seemed full of fire and courage and life, but at heart he was cold and almost a coward, until his vanity was touched, then he would not stop at anything.... And really when I recall our gatherings, upon my word there was much that was fine, even touching in them.... Ah, that was a glorious time, and I can't bear to believe that it was altogether wasted! And it was not wasted—not even for those whose lives were sordid afterwards. How often have I chanced to come across such old college friends! You would think the man had sunk altogether to the brute, but one had only to utter Pokorsky's name before him and every trace of noble feeling in him was stirred at once; it was like uncorking a forgotten phial of fragrance in some dark and dirty room.'"

How perfect is the form of the novel! Rudin's sudden appearance at Darya Mihailovna's house, from the void, his brief, brilliant scintillation, his disappearance beyond the horizon like a falling star, while the little circle he has quitted returns to its quiet settled round, and is knitted closer, by and by, in two marriages. In the final chapters Turgenev gives a wonderful feeling of the stormy horizon of life in his glimpses of Rudin's restless wanderings, of his pathetic series of failures, of his useless death in a hopeless cause on a Paris barricade. It is now the genius of Turgenev's heart that speaks, the head in absolute unison with the heart. For Turgenev's creative judgment, infinitely just, infinitely tender, is a court of appeal from all hard, worldly arraignments. All that has been shown us of Rudin's Utopianism, of the "something lacking" in his character and outlook is true. But it is not the whole truth. In Lezhnyov's final words, "Rudin has faith, Rudin has honesty. He has enthusiasm, the most precious quality in our times. We have all become insufferably reasonable and indifferent and slothful." That is the point. The Rudins, the idealists of the "'forties," were the yeast in the dough of Russian fatalism and the nation's stagnation. For one idealist there were a thousand lethargic, acquiescent minds, clinging to the rock of personal interest, staking nothing, but all subservient to the forces of official despotism or worldly power. In Rudin burned clear the light of humane, generous ideals, of the fire of the love of truth. Most of the intellectual seed he scattered fell by the wayside or was swallowed up in the morass of Russia's social distress and mass impotence. But, in Lezhnyov's words: "I say again, that is not Rudin's fault, and it is his fate—a cruel and unhappy fate—for which we cannot blame him." And when we survey the figures of that gloomy reign of Nicholas, when "a merciless Imperialism repressed the least sign of intellectuality," it was the Rudins who breathed on and passed on that living seed of fire to the younger generation.

It is to be remarked that not a line, not a detail in the social picture seems to have faded. The picture by its truth and art is timeless in its plastic grace, like a Tanagra group, or a Velasquez portrait. Nothing, indeed, can be added or taken away from the masterpiece.

V
"A HOUSE OF GENTLEFOLK"

CHAPTER V

"A HOUSE OF GENTLEFOLK"

In 1859, three years after *Rudin*, appeared *A House of Gentlefolk*, in popular estimation the most perfect of Turgenev's works. This verdict, repeated by many critics, was gained no less by the pathos of Lavretsky's love story than by the faultless character drawing, the gentle, earnest, religious Liza[16] being balanced against the voluptuous, worldly coquette, Varvara Pavlovna. The story which chronicles how the latter, *la belle Madame de Lavretsky*, twists her honest, candid husband round her finger, how at length Lavretsky discovers her infidelities, and returns to Russia where he meets and falls in love with Liza, and how, on the false news of his wife's death, they confess their mutual passion—when their dream is shattered by the dramatic reappearance of Varvara Pavlovna—is characteristic of Turgenev's underlying sad philosophy.

[16] Liza, "the best impersonation possible of the average, thoroughly good and honest Russian girl of the times."—KROPOTKIN.

Both Turgenev's temperamental melancholy and irony are seconded by, indeed are enrooted in, his calm, piercing perception of the ineffectual struggle of virtue in the vortex of worldly power. All the great literature of all the ages warns us that the world is mainly swayed by force and craft, twin children of human necessity and appetite. Virtue, beautiful in its disinterested impulse, as the love of truth, has always to reckon with the all-powerful law of life, self-interest, on which the whole fabric of society is reared. Goodness is but a frail defence against the designs of force and egoistic craft. We see magnanimity falling before unscrupulousness; while the stupidity of the mass of men is twisted adroitly by the worldly to their own advantage. While Turgenev's philosophy reinforces the experience of the ages, his pictures of life are distinguished by the subtle spiritual light which plays upon the egoistic basis. In his vision "the rack of this tough world" triumphs, but his peculiarly subtle appeal to our sense of spiritual beauty registers the common earthiness of the triumph of force and evil. That triumph is everywhere; it is a fundamental law of nature that worldly craft and appetite shall prevail, whelming the finer forces, but Turgenev's sadness and irony, by their beauty of feeling, strengthen those spiritual valuations which challenge the elemental law. His aesthetic method is so to place in juxtaposition the fine shades of human worldliness that we enjoy the spectacle of the varied strands composing a family or social pattern. In the sketch of Lavretsky's ancestors, for two generations, the pattern is intricate, surprisingly varied, giving us the richest sense of all the heterogeneous elements that combine in a family stock. In the portraits of Varvara Pavlovna's father and mother we recognize the lines of heredity:

> "Varvara Pavlovna's father, Pavel Petrovitch Korobyin, a retired major-general, had spent his whole time on duty in Petersburg. He had had the reputation in his youth of a good dancer and driller. Through poverty he had served as adjutant to two or three generals of no distinction, and had married the daughter of one of them with a dowry of twenty-five thousand roubles. He mastered all the science of military discipline and manoeuvres to the minutest niceties, he went on in harness, till at last, after twenty-five years' service, he received the rank of a general and the command of a regiment. Then he might have relaxed his efforts and quietly secured his pecuniary position. Indeed this was what he reckoned upon doing, but he managed things a little incautiously. He devised a new method of speculating with public funds—the method seemed an excellent one in itself—but he neglected to bribe in the right place and was consequently informed against, and a more than unpleasant, a disgraceful scandal followed ... he was advised to retire from active duty.... His bald head, with its tufts of dyed hair, and the soiled ribbon of the order of St. Anne, which he wore over a cravat of the colour of a raven's wing, began to be familiar to all the pale and listless young men who hang morosely about the card-tables while dancing is going on. Pavel Petrovitch knew how to gain a footing in society; he spoke little, but from long habit, condescendingly—though of course not when he was talking to persons of a higher rank than his own.... Of the general's wife there is scarcely anything to be said. Kalliopa Karlovna, who was of German extraction, considered herself a woman of great sensibility. She was always in a state of nervous agitation, seemed as though she were ill-nourished, and wore a tight velvet dress, a cap, and tarnished hollow bracelets."

In this incisive little cameo Turgenev has told us everything about Varvara Pavlovna's upbringing. It is typical of Turgenev's method, of indicating with sparse, magic touches the *couche sociale*, so that we see working in the individual the forces that form him as a social type. Varvara Pavlovna, in her arts, is the worldly woman incarnate, sensual in her cold, polished being, in her luxurious elegance, in her inherently vulgar ambition. But Turgenev's instinctive *justesse* is shown in the attractiveness of Varvara Pavlovna's bodily beauty. Remark that the more Turgenev unmasks her coldness and falsity the more he renders tribute to her bodily charm, to the subtle intelligence in her dark, oval, lovely face, with its splendid eyes, which gazed softly and attentively from under her fine brows. She is a worldly syren, lovely and desirable in her sensual fascination. But she is not too discriminating in the choice of her male adorers. His remembrance of all her deceptions stings Lavretsky when in her manœuvres to be reinstated in society she descends upon him suddenly at O——:

> "The first thing that struck him as he went into the entrance hall was a scent of patchouli, always distasteful to him; there were some high travelling-trunks standing there. The face of his groom, who ran out to meet him, seemed strange to him. Not stopping to analyse his impressions, he crossed the threshold of the drawing-room.... On his entrance there rose from the sofa a lady in a black silk dress with flounces, who, raising a cambric handkerchief to her pale face, made a few paces forward, bent her carefully dressed, perfumed head, and fell at his feet.... Then, only, he recognised her: this lady was his wife!
>
> "He caught his breath.... He leaned against the wall.
>
> "'*Théodore*, do not repulse me!' she said in French, and her voice cut to his heart like a knife.
>
> "He looked at her senselessly, and yet he noticed involuntarily at once that she had grown both whiter and fatter.
>
> "'*Théodore!*' she went on, from time to time lifting her eyes and discreetly wringing her marvellously beautiful fingers with their rosy, polished nails. '*Théodore*, I have wronged you, deeply wronged you; I will say more, I have sinned; but hear me; I am tortured by remorse, I have grown hateful to myself, I could endure my position no longer; how many times have I thought of turning to you, but I feared your anger; I resolved to break every tie with the past.... *Puis, j'ai été si malade*.... I have been so ill,' she added, and passed her hand over her brow and cheek. 'I took advantage of the widely-spread rumour of my death, I gave up everything; without resting day or night I hastened hither; I hesitated long to appear before you, my judge ... *paraître devant vous, mon juge*; but I resolved at last, remembering your constant goodness, to come to you; I found your address at Moscow. Believe me,' she went on, slowly getting up from the floor

and sitting on the very edge of an armchair. 'I have often thought of death, and I should have found courage to take my life ... ah! life is a burden unbearable for me now!... but the thought of my daughter, my little Ada, stopped me. She is here, she is asleep in the next room, the poor child! She is tired—you shall see her; she at least has done you no wrong, and I am so unhappy, so unhappy!' cried Madame Lavretsky, and she melted into tears....

"... 'I have no commands to give you,' replied Lavretsky in the same colourless voice; 'you know, all is over between us ... and now more than ever; you can live where you like; and if your allowance is too little——'

"'Ah, don't say such dreadful things,' Varvara Pavlovna interrupted him, 'spare me, if only ... if only for the sake of this angel.' And as she uttered these words, Varvara Pavlovna ran impulsively into the next room, and returned at once with a small and very elegantly dressed little girl in her arms. Thick flaxen curls fell over her pretty rosy little face, and on to her large sleepy black eyes; she smiled, and blinked her eyes at the light and laid a chubby little hand on her mother's neck.

"'Ada, *vois, c'est ton père,*' said Varvara Pavlovna, pushing the curls back from her eyes and kissing her vigorously, '*prie-le avec moi.*'

"'*C'est ça, papa?*' stammered the little girl lisping.

"'*Oui, mon enfant, n'est-ce pas que tu l'aimes?*'

"But this was more than Lavretsky could stand.

"'In what melodrama is there a scene exactly like this?' he muttered and went out of the room.

"Varvara Pavlovna stood still for some time in the same place, slightly shrugged her shoulders, carried the little girl off into the next room, undressed her and put her to bed. Then she took up a book and sat down near the lamp, and after staying up for an hour she went to bed herself.

"'*Eh bien, madame?*' queried her maid, a French woman whom she had brought from Paris, as she unlaced her corset.

"'*Eh bien, Justine,*' she replied, 'he is a good deal older, but I fancy he is just the same good-natured fellow. Give me my gloves for the night, and get out my grey, high-necked dress for to-morrow, and don't forget the mutton cutlets for Ada.... I daresay it will be difficult to get them here; but we must try.'

"'*A la guerre comme à la guerre,*' replied Justine, as she put out the candle."

The reader should contrast with the above satiric passage, the summer evening scene in the garden at Vassilyevskoe (chap. xxvi.), where Marya Dmitrievna's party sit by the pond fishing. The soft tranquillity of the hour, the charm of this pure young girl, Liza, with "her soft, glowing cheeks and somewhat severe profile" as "she looked at the water, half frowning, to keep the sun out of her eyes, half smiling," the tender evening atmosphere, all are faintly stirred, like the rippling surface of a stream, by a puff of wind, by Liza's words upon her religious thoughts on death. In this delicate, glancing conversation, Turgenev while mirroring, as in a glass, the growing intimacy of feeling between Liza and Lavretsky, discloses almost imperceptibly the sunken rock on which his happiness is to strike and suffer shipwreck—Liza's profound instinct of self-abnegation and self-sacrifice. Her sweet seriousness, her slowness of brain, her very lack of words, all appear to Lavretsky enchanting. This scene in the garden, in its tender breathing tranquillity, holds suspended beneath the gentle, flowing stream of the lovers' happiness, the faint, ambiguous menace of the days to come.

In depicting the contest between Varvara Pavlovna's worldliness and Liza's spirituality, how comes it that Turgenev's *parti pris* for Liza has not impaired the aesthetic balance? It is because he shows us how Lavretsky's mistake in marrying this syren has tied his hands. The forces of worldly convention when reinforced by Liza's religious conviction that Varvara Pavlovna, odious as she is, is still Lavretsky's wife, are bound to triumph. Accordingly the more the all-pervasive, all-conquering force of worldliness is done justice to, and the more its brilliant, polished appearances are displayed in all their deceptive colours, *the greater is our reaction towards spiritual beauty.* Therefore Turgenev, with his unerring instinct, intersperses Liza's sad love story with scenes of the brilliant worldly comedy played between that *comme-il-faut* pair, Panshin, the brilliant young official from Petersburg, Liza's suitor, and Varvara Pavlovna.

Turgenev sees through the pretences of his worldly types at a glance. All the inflexions of their engaging manners reflect as in a clear mirror the evasive shades of their worldly motives. He has a peculiar gift of so contrasting their tones of insincerity that the artificial pattern of their intercourse gleams and glistens in its polished falsity. As a social comedy of the purest water, how delightful are the scenes where the foolish Marya Dmitrievna, the old counsellor Gedeonovsky, and Panshin with his diplomatic reserve, are fascinated by the seductive modesty of Varvara Pavlovna (chap. xxxix.). How natural in the interplay of ironic light and shade is the picture of Varvara Pavlovna's conquest of her provincial audience. Note, moreover, how in art and literature and music, what always thrills these ladies and gentlemen is the polished, insipid, *chic morceau*. Their talk, their manner, their aspiration are all of the surface, facile, smooth polished, like their scented, white hands, and one listens to their correctly modulated voices exchanging compliments and social banalities, suavely, in the reception room, while beneath this correct surface is self, self and worldly advantage. That is the one reality. The world of beautiful feeling, of disinterested, generous impulse, is on quite another plane; it is as strange and alien to their minds as the peasant's rough, harsh world of labour. Examine the exact relation Panshin bears to the world in which he is so successfully playing his part:

> "Panshin's father, a retired cavalry officer and a notorious gambler, was a man with insinuating eyes, a battered countenance, and a nervous twitch about the mouth. He spent his whole life hanging about the aristocratic world; frequented the English clubs of both capitals, and had the reputation of a smart, not very trustworthy, but jolly good-natured fellow. In spite of his smartness, he was almost always on the brink of ruin, and the property he left his son was small and heavily encumbered. To make up for that, however, he did exert himself, after his own fashion, over his son's education. Vladimir Nikolaitch spoke French very well, English well, and German badly; that is the proper thing: fashionable people would be ashamed to speak German well; but to utter an occasional—generally a humorous—phrase in German is quite correct, *c'est même très chic*, as the Parisians of Petersburg express themselves. By the time he was fifteen, Vladimir knew how to enter any drawing-room without embarrassment, how to move about in it gracefully and to leave it at the appropriate moment. Panshin's father gained many connections for his son. He never lost an opportunity, while shuffling the cards between two rubbers, or playing a successful trump, of dropping a hint about his Volodka to any personage of importance who was a devotee of cards. And Vladimir, too, during his residence at the University, which he left without a very brilliant degree, formed an acquaintance with several young

men of quality, and gained an entry into the best houses. He was received cordially everywhere: he was very good-looking, easy in his manners, amusing, always in good health, and ready for everything; respectful, when he ought to be; insolent, when he dared to be; excellent company, *un charmant garçon*. The promised land lay before him. Panshin quickly learnt the secret of getting on in the world; he knew how to yield with genuine respect to its decrees; he knew how to take up trifles with half ironical seriousness, and to appear to regard everything serious as trifling; he was a capital dancer; and dressed in the English style. In a short time he gained the reputation of being one of the smartest and most attractive young men in Petersburg. Panshin was indeed very smart, not less so than his father; but he was also very talented. He did everything well; he sang charmingly, sketched with spirit, wrote verses, and was a very fair actor. He was only twenty-eight, and he was already a *Kammer-Yunker*, and he had a very good position. Panshin had complete confidence in himself, in his own intelligence, and his own penetration; he made his way with light-hearted assurance, everything went smoothly with him. He was used to being liked by everyone, old and young, and imagined he understood people, especially women: he certainly understood their ordinary weaknesses. As a man of artistic leanings, he was conscious of a capacity for passion, for being carried away, even for enthusiasm, and, consequently, he permitted himself various irregularities; he was dissipated, associated with persons not belonging to good society, and, in general, conducted himself in a free and easy manner; but at heart he was cold and false, and at the moment of the most boisterous revelry his sharp brown eye was always alert, taking everything in. This bold, independent young man could never forget himself and be completely carried away. To his credit it must be said, that he never boasted of his conquests."

The passage we have cited illustrates Turgenev's method of so placing in perspective the fine shades of worldliness that their social significance is seen contrasted with the force of spiritual beauty beyond, out of their ken. Panshin cannot but rise in the world, for his polished astuteness is weakened by no feeling of mental integrity, his coldness is impaired by no sympathy with merit which is unsuccessful. In official life as in society Panshin is the type of the *arriviste*, and his "Western" liberal sympathies, one knows, are part of the flowing tide; otherwise Panshin would not be expressing them. In ten years later the official tide will be flowing the other way, and Panshin, more dignified and stouter, with the Vladimir Cross on his frock-coated breast, will be emphasizing the necessity for severer measures of Governmental reaction. The Panshins are legion.

To reveal Panshin's essence in his actions Turgenev employs but a single stroke—Panshin's spitefulness to the old music-master, Lemm, a musician of genius, but solitary, poor and despised because "he did not know how to set about things in the right way, to gain favour in the right place, and to make a push at the right moment." Lemm has composed for his pupil, Liza, a religious cantata. Panshin has seen the score, inscribed "For you alone," and for the pleasure of mortifying the old man who has called him a dilettante, he twits Lemm about the composition, thereby betraying the young girl's confidence:

> "... Liza's eyes were fixed directly on Panshin, and expressed displeasure. There was no smile on her lips, her whole face looked stern and even mournful.
>
> "'What's the matter?' he asked.
>
> "'Why did you not keep your word?' she said. 'I showed you Christopher Fedoritch's cantata on the express condition that you said nothing about it to him.'
>
> "'I beg your pardon, Lisaveta Mihalovna, the words slipped out unawares.'
>
> "'You have hurt his feelings and mine too. Now he will not trust even me.'
>
> "'How could I help it, Lisaveta Mihalovna? Ever since I was a little boy I could never see a German without wanting to tease him.'
>
> "'How can you say that, Vladimir Nikolaitch? This German is poor, lonely, and broken-down—have you no pity for him? Can you wish to tease him?'
>
> "Panshin was taken aback.
>
> "'You are right, Lisaveta Mihalovna,' he declared. 'It's my everlasting thoughtlessness that's to blame. No, don't contradict me; I know myself. So much harm has come to me from my want of thought. It's owing to that failing that I am thought to be an egoist.'

> "Panshin paused. With whatever subject he began a conversation, he generally ended by talking of himself, and the subject was changed by him so easily, so smoothly and genially, that it seemed unconscious."

Thus delicately Turgenev indicates the impassable spiritual gulf between Panshin and the pure, serious Liza. It is an illustration of Turgenev's genius in disclosing life as a constantly growing, changing phenomenon. His artistic synthesis reproduces all the hesitating inflexions in Liza's feeling, and soon the interest that, as an inexperienced girl, she takes in Panshin's attentions will fade before the mounting wave of Lavretsky's love.

The sequel our readers have divined, if they do not already know *A House of Gentlefolk*. We have seen above how Varvara Pavlovna's return from the void, blights Lavretsky's future; and now through the closing chapters, xliii. to xlv., of the worldly comedy of her social rehabilitation, sounds the low, piercing note of Liza's renunciation. For her the convent, for Lavretsky henceforward his unavailing memories. It is the idealistic girl, who at the Church's behest, immolates herself and the man she loves on the altar of her religion. And Varvara Pavlovna is left softly smiling at Lavretsky's inner misery; and "the day after his departure, Panshin appeared at Lavricky, the lofty apartments of the house, and even the garden re-echoed with the sound of music, singing and lively French talk—and Panshin, when he took leave of Varvara Pavlovna, warmly pressing her lovely hands, promised to come back very soon—and he kept his word."

It is life, and to those who rebel against the innocent bearing the sorrow of renunciation, Turgenev addresses the beautiful Epilogue in which we see Lavretsky, years later, revisiting the house of Marya Dmitrievna now dead and gone, and sitting alone in the room where he had so often looked at Liza, he hears the happy laughter of the young, careless people, the young generation, ringing in the sunlit garden:

> "Lavretsky quietly rose and quietly went away; no one noticed him, no one detained him; the joyous cries sounded more loudly in the garden behind the thick green wall of high lime trees. He took his seat in the carriage and bade the coachman drive home and not hurry the horses.... They say, Lavretsky visited that convent where Liza had hidden herself—that he saw her. Crossing over from choir to choir, she walked close past him, moving with the even, hurried, but meek walk of a nun; and she did not glance at him; only the eyelashes on the side towards him quivered a little, only she bent her emaciated face lower, and the fingers of her

clasped hands, entwined with her rosary, were pressed still closer to one another. What were they both thinking? What were they feeling? Who can know? Who can say? There are such moments in life, there are such feelings.... One can but point to them—and pass by."

VI
"ON THE EVE"

CHAPTER VI

"ON THE EVE"

On the Eve, not finished and published till 1859, but projected in 1855, and then laid aside for *Rudin* and *A House of Gentlefolk*, holds depths of meaning which at first sight lie veiled under the simple harmonious surface. To the English reader *On the Eve* is a charming picture of a quiet Russian household, with a delicate analysis of a young girl's soul. For Russians, however, on the background is cast the wavering shadow of Russia's national aspirations.

Elena, the heroine, as Turgenev tells us, was "a new type in Russian life," when his idea of her first began to trouble his imagination; but "I could not find the hero to whom she, with her vague but strong aspirations for liberty, could give herself." In comparing her with Natalya and Liza the reader will remark that he is allowed to come into even closer spiritual contact with her than with them. When Elena stands before us we know the innermost secrets of her character. Her strength of will, her serious, courageous, proud soul, her capacity for passion, all the play of her idealistic nature troubled by the contradictions, aspirations, and unhappiness that the dawn of love brings to her, all this is conveyed to us by a simple and consummate art. The diary (chap. xvi.) that Elena keeps is in itself a masterly revelation of a young girl's heart; it has never been equalled by any other novelist.

How exquisitely Turgenev reveals his characters may be seen by an examination of the parts Shubin the artist, and Bersenyev the student, play towards Elena. Both young men are in love with her, and the description of their after relations as friends, and the feelings of Elena towards them, and her own self-communings are interwoven with unfaltering skill. All the most complex and baffling shades of the mental life, in the hands of Turgenev are used with deftness and certainty to bring to light the complexity of motives and instincts which is always lying hidden beneath the surface, beneath the commonplace of daily life. In the difficult art of literary perspective, in the effective grouping of contrasts in character and the criss-cross of the influence of the different individuals, lies one of the secrets of Turgenev's supremacy. As an example the reader may note how he is made to judge Elena through six pairs of eyes—Stahov's contempt for his daughter, her mother's affectionate bewilderment, Shubin's petulant criticism, Bersenyev's half-hearted enthralment, Insarov's recognition, and Zoya's indifference, being the facets for converging light on Elena's sincerity and depth of soul. Again one may note Turgenev's method for rehabilitating Shubin in our eyes; Shubin is simply made to criticise Stahov; the thing is done in a few seemingly careless lines, but these lines lay bare Shubin's strength and weakness, the fluidity of his nature. The reader who does not see the art which underlies almost every line of *On the Eve* is merely paying the highest tribute to that art; as often the clear waters of a pool conceal its surprising depth. Taking Shubin's character as an example of creative skill, we cannot call to mind any instance in the range of European fiction where the typical artist mind, on its lighter sides, has been analysed with such delicacy and truth as here by Turgenev. The irresponsibility, alertness, the whimsicality and mobility of Shubin combine to charm and irritate the reader in the exact proportion that such a character affects him in actual life; there is not the least touch of exaggeration, and all the values are kept to a marvel. Looking at the minor characters, perhaps one may say that the father of Elena will be the most suggestive, and not the least familiar character, to English households. His essentially masculine meanness, his self-complacency, his unconscious indifference to the opinion of others, his absurdity as *un père de famille*, are balanced by the foolish affection and jealousy which his wife, Anna Vassilyevna, cannot help feeling towards him. The perfect balance and duality of Turgenev's outlook are here shown by the equal cleverness with which he seizes on and quietly derides the typical masculine and typical feminine attitude in such a married life as the Stahovs'.

Turning to the figure of the Bulgarian hero, it is interesting to find from the *Souvenirs sur Tourguénev* (published in 1887) that Turgenev's only distinct failure of importance in character drawing, Insarov, was not taken from life, but was the legacy of a friend, Karateieff, who implored Turgenev to work out an unfinished conception. Insarov is a figure of wood. He is so cleverly constructed, and the central idea behind him so strong, that his wooden joints move naturally, and the spectator has only the instinct, not the certainty, of being cheated. The idea he incarnates, that of a man whose soul is aflame with patriotism, is finely suggested, but an idea, even a great one, does not make an individuality. And, in fact, Insarov is not a man, he is an automaton. To compare Shubin's utterances with his is to perceive that there is no spontaneity, no inevitability in Insarov. He is a patriotic clock wound up to go for the occasion, and in truth he is very useful. Only on his deathbed, when the unexpected happens, and the machinery runs down, do we feel moved. Then he appears more striking dead than alive—a rather damning testimony to the power Turgenev credits him with. This artistic failure of Turgenev's is, as he no doubt recognized, curiously lessened by the fact that young girls of Elena's lofty idealistic type are particularly impressed by certain stiff types of men of action and great will-power, whose capacity for moving straight towards a goal by no means implies corresponding brain-power. The insight of a Shubin and the moral worth of a Bersenyev are not so valuable to the Elenas of this world, whose ardent desire to be made good use of, and to seek some great end, is best developed by strength of aim in the men they love.

And now to see what the novel before us meant to the contemporary Russian mind, we must turn to the infinitely suggestive background. Turgenev's genius was of the same force in politics as in art; it was that of seeing aright. He saw his country as it was, with clearer eyes than any man before or since. As a critic of his generation little escaped Turgenev's eye, as a politician he foretold nearly all that actually came to pass in his life, and as a consummate artist, led first and foremost by his love for his art, his novels are undying historical pictures. It is not that there is anything allegorical in his novels—allegory is at the farthest pole from his method; it is that whenever he created an important figure in fiction that figure is necessarily a revelation of the secrets of the fatherland, the soil, the race. Turgenev, in short, was a psychologist not merely of men, but of nations; and so the chief figure of *On the Eve*, Elena, foreshadows and stands for the rise of Young Russia in the 'sixties. Elena is Young Russia, and to whom does she turn in her prayer for strength? Not to Bersenyev, the philosopher, the dreamer; not to Shubin, the man carried outside himself by every passing distraction; but to the strong man, Insarov. And here the irony of Insarov being made a foreigner, a Bulgarian, is significant of Turgenev's distrust of his country's weakness. The hidden meaning of the novel is a cry to the coming men to unite their strength against the foe without and the foe within the gates; it is not only an appeal to them to hasten the death of the old régime of Nicholas I., but an appeal to them to conquer their sluggishness, their weakness and their apathy. It is a cry for Men. Turgenev sought in vain in life for a type of man to satisfy Russia, and ended by taking no living model for his hero, but the hearsay Insarov, a foreigner. Russia has not yet produced men of this type. But the artist does not despair of the future. Here we come upon one of the most striking figures of Turgenev—that of Uvar Ivanovitch. He symbolizes the ever-predominant type of Russian, the sleepy, the slothful Slav of yesterday. He is the Slav whose inherent force Europe is as ignorant of as he is himself. Though he speaks only twenty sentences in the book he is a creation of Tolstoian force. His very words are dark and of practically no significance. There lies the irony of the social picture. On the eve of what? one asks. Time has given contradictory answers to the men of all parties. The Elenas of to-day need not turn their eyes abroad to find their counterpart in spirit; so far at least the pessimists are refuted; but the note of death that Turgenev strikes in his marvellous chapter on Venice has still for Young Russia an ominous echo—so many generations have arisen eager, only to be flung aside helpless, that one asks, what of the generation that fronts Autocracy to-day?[17]

[17] Written in 1895.

> "'Do you remember I asked you, "Will there ever be men among us?" and you answered, "There will be." O primæval force! And now from here in "my poetic distance" I will ask you again, "What do you say, Uvar Ivanovitch, will there be?"'
>
> "Uvar Ivanovitch flourished his fingers, and fixed his enigmatical stare into the far distance."

This creation of a universal national type, out of the flesh and blood of a fat, taciturn country gentleman, brings us to see that Turgenev was not merely an artist, but that he was a poet using fiction as his medium. To this end it is instructive to compare Jane Austen, perhaps the greatest English exponent of the domestic novel, with the Russian master, and to note that, while her picture of manners is as indestructible as his, she is absolutely wanting in his poetic insight. How petty and parochial appears her outlook in *Emma*, compared with Turgenev's wide and unflinching gaze. She painted most admirably the English types she knew, and how well she knew them! but she failed to correlate them with the national life; and yet, while her men and women were acting and thinking, Trafalgar and Waterloo were being fought and won. But each of Turgenev's novels in some subtle way suggests that the people he introduces are playing their little part in a great national drama everywhere round us, invisible, yet audible through the clamour of voices near us. And so *On the Eve*, the work of a poet, has certain deep notes, which break through the harmonious tenor of the whole, and strangely and swiftly transfigure the quiet story, troubling us with a dawning consciousness of the march of mighty events. Suddenly a strange sense steals upon the reader that he is living in a perilous atmosphere, filling his heart with foreboding, and enveloping at length the characters themselves, all unconsciously awaiting disaster in the sunny woods and gardens of Kuntsevo. But not till the last chapters are reached does the English reader perceive that in recreating for him the mental atmosphere of a single educated Russian household, Turgenev has been casting before his eyes the faint shadow of the national drama which was indeed played, though left unfinished, on the Balkan battlefields of 1876-77. Briefly, Turgenev, in sketching the dawn of love in a young girl's soul, has managed faintly, but unmistakably, to make spring and flourish in our minds the ineradicable, though hidden, idea at the back of Slav thought—the unification of the Slav races.

How doubly welcome that art should be which can lead us, the foreigner, thus straight to the heart of the national secrets of a great people, secrets which our own critics and diplomatists have so often misrepresented. Each of Turgenev's novels may be said to contain a light-bringing rejoinder to the old-fashioned criticism of the Muscovite, current up to the rise of the great Russian novel, and still, unfortunately, lingering among us;[18] but *On the Eve*, of all the novels, contains, perhaps, the most instructive political lesson England can learn. Europe has always had, and most assuredly England has been very rich in those alarm-monger critics, watchdogs for ever baying at Slav cupidity, treachery, intrigue, and so on and so on. It is useful to have these well-meaning animals on the political premises, giving noisy tongue whenever the Slav stretches out his long arm and opens his drowsy eyes, but how rare it is to find a man who can teach us to interpret a nation's aspirations, to gauge its inner force, its aim, its inevitability. Turgenev gives us such clues. In the respectful, if slightly forced, silence that has been imposed by certain recent political events[19] on the tribe of faithful watchdogs, it may be permitted to one to say, that whatever England's interest may be in relation to Russia's development, it is better for us to understand the force of Russian aims before we measure our strength against it. And a novel, such as *On the Eve*, though now it is nearly forty years old, and to the short-sighted out of date, reveals in a flash the attitude of the Slav towards his political destiny. His aspirations may have to slumber through policy or necessity; they may be distorted or misrepresented, or led astray by official action, but we confess for us *On the Eve* suggests the existence of a mighty lake, whose waters, dammed back for a while, are rising slowly, but are still some way from the brim. How long will it take to the overflow? Nobody knows; but when the long winter of Russia's dark internal policy shall be broken up, will the snows, melting on the mountains, stream southwest, inundating the valley of the Danube? Or, as the national poet, Pushkin, has sung, will there be a pouring of many Slavonian rivulets into the Russian sea, a powerful attraction of the Slav races towards a common centre to create an era of peace and development within, whereby Russia may rise free and rejoicing to face her great destinies? Hard and bitter is the shaping of nations. Uvar Ivanovitch still fixes his enigmatical stare into the far distance.

[18] Passages written in 1895.

[19] Passages written in 1895.

Twenty-two years ago the above appreciation of *On the Eve* was written by the present writer, who, on re-reading it, finds it necessary to alter only two or three sentences. The sentence "The respectful, if slightly forced, silence that has been imposed by recent political events on the tribe of faithful watchdogs" is an allusion to the first attempt made by our diplomatists and our Court, on the accession of Nicholas II., to reverse the traditional policy of England's hostility to Russia. The sequel, despite the surprising ups and downs of the political barometer, was determined by Germany's naval policy and the Anglo-French *entente*.

VII
"FATHERS AND CHILDREN"

CHAPTER VII

"FATHERS AND CHILDREN"

I

While *On the Eve* signalizes the end of the Crimea epoch and the break-up of the crushing, overwhelming régime of Nicholas, *Fathers and Children* is a forecast of the new Liberal movement which arose in the Russia of the 'sixties, and an analysis of the formidable type appearing on the political horizon—the Nihilist.

Turgenev was the first man to detect the existence of this new type, the Nihilist. His own account of his discovery gives us such an interesting glimpse of his method in creative work that we transcribe a passage from his paper on *Fathers and Children*, written at Baden in 1869:

> "It was in the month of August 1860, when I was taking sea baths at Ventnor, in the Isle of Wight, that the first idea of *Fathers and Children* came into my head; that novel, thanks to which the favourable opinion of the younger generation about me, has come to an end. Many times I have heard and read in critical journals that I have only been elaborating an idea of my own.... For my part, I ought to confess that I never attempted to create a type without having, not an idea, but a living person, in whom the various elements were harmonised together, to work from. I have always needed some groundwork on which I could tread firmly. This was the case with *Fathers and Children*. At the foundation of the principal figure Bazarov was the personality of a young provincial doctor. He died not long before 1860. In that remarkable man was incarnated to my ideas the just rising element, which, still chaotic, afterwards received the title of Nihilism. The impression produced by this individual was very strong. At first I could not clearly define him to myself. But I strained my eyes and ears, watching everything surrounding me, anxious to trust simply in my own sensations. What confounded me was that I had met not a single idea or hint of what seemed appearing to me on all sides. And the doubt involuntarily suggested itself...."

Fathers and Children was published in the spring of 1862 in Katkoff's paper, *The Russian Messenger*, the organ of the Younger Generation, and the stormy controversy that the novel immediately provoked was so bitter, deep and lasting that the episode forms one of the most interesting chapters in literary history. Rarely has so great an artist so thoroughly drawn public attention to a scrutiny of new ideas rising in its midst; rarely has so great an artist come into such violent collision with his own party thereby; never, perhaps, has there been so striking an illustration of the incapacity of the public, swayed by party passion, to understand a pure work of art. The effect of the publication was widespread excitement in both political camps. Everybody was, at the time, on the alert to see what would be the next move on the political board. The recent Emancipation of the Serfs was looked upon by Young Russia as only the prelude to many democratic measures, while the Reactionists professed to see in that measure the ruin of the country and the beginning of the end. The fast-increasing antipathy between the Old Order and the New, like a fire, required only a puff of wind to set it ablaze. And Bazarov's character and aims came as a godsend to the Reactionists, who hailed in it the portrait of the insidious revolutionary ideas current in Young Russia; and they hastened to crowd round Turgenev, ironically congratulating the former champion of Liberalism on his penetration and honesty in unmasking the Nihilist. But we will quote Turgenev's own words:

> "I will not enlarge on the effect produced by this novel. I will only say that everywhere the word Nihilist was caught up by a thousand tongues, and that on the day of the conflagration of the Apraksinsky shops, when I arrived in St. Petersburg, the first exclamation with which I was greeted was, 'Just see what your Nihilists are doing!' ... I experienced a coldness approaching to indignation from people near and sympathetic to me. I received congratulations, almost caresses, from people of the opposite camp, from enemies. This confused me, wounded me; but my conscience did not reproach me. I knew very well I had carried out honestly the type I had sketched, carried it out not only without prejudice, but positively with sympathy.... While some attack me for outraging the Younger Generation, and promise me, with a laugh of contempt, to burn my photograph, others, on the contrary, with indignation, reproach me for my servile cringing to the Younger Generation.... 'You are grovelling at the feet of Bazarov. You pretend to find fault with him, and you are licking the dust at his feet,' says one correspondent. Another critic represented M. Katkoff and me as two conspirators, 'plotting in the solitude of our chamber our traps and slanders against the forces of Young Russia.' An effective picture!... My critics called my work a pamphlet, and referred to my wounded and irritated vanity.... A

shadow has fallen on my name. I don't deceive myself. I know that shadow will remain."

Politics is a game where the mistakes and admissions of your adversary are your good character in public opinion—a definition which goes far to account for the easy predominance of the political sharper,—and so Turgenev, the great artist, he who, in creating Bazarov for an ungrateful public, to use his own words, "*simply did not know how to work otherwise,*" found to his cost. The Younger Generation, irritated by the public capital made out of Bazarov and his Nihilism by "the Fathers," flew into the other extreme, and refused to see in Bazarov anything other than a *caricature* of itself. It denied Bazarov was of its number, or represented its views in any way; and to this day surviving Nihilists will demonstrate warmly that the creation of his sombre figure is "a mistake from beginning to end." The reason for this wholesale rejection of Bazarov is easy to account for; and Turgenev, whose clear-sightedness about his works was unaffected either by vanity, diffidence or the ignorant onslaughts of the whole tribe of minor critics, penetrates at once to the heart of the matter:

> "The whole ground of the misunderstanding lay in the fact that the type of Bazarov had not time to pass through the usual phases. At the very moment of his appearance the author attacked him. It was a new method as well as a new type I introduced—that of Realizing instead of Idealizing.... The reader is easily thrown into perplexity when the author does not show clear sympathy or antipathy to his own child. The reader readily gets angry.... After all, books exist to entertain."

An excellent piece of analysis and a quiet piece of irony this! The character of Bazarov was in fact such an epitome of the depths of a great movement that the mass of commonplace educated minds, the future tools of the movement, looked on it with alarm, dislike and dread. The average man will only recognize his own qualities in his fellows, and endow a man with his own littlenesses. So Bazarov's depth excited the superficiality of the eternally omnipresent average mind. The Idealists in the Younger Generation were mortally grieved to see that Bazarov was not wholly inspired by their dreams; he went deeper, and the average man received a shock of surprise that hurt his vanity. So the hue and cry was raised around Turgenev, and raised only too well. Bazarov is the most dominating of Turgenev's creations, yet it brought upon him secret distrust and calumny, undermined his influence with those he was with at heart, and went far to damage his position as the leading novelist of his day. The lesson is significant. No generation ever understands itself; its members welcome eagerly their portraits drawn by their friends, and the caricatures drawn by their adversaries; but to the new type no mercy is shown, and everybody hastens to misunderstand, to abuse, to destroy.

So widely indeed was Bazarov misunderstood that Turgenev once asserted, "At this very moment there are only two people who have understood my intentions—Dostoevsky and Botkin."

And Dostoevsky was of the opposite camp—a Slavophil.

II

What, then, is Bazarov?

Time after time Turgenev took the opportunity, now in an article, now in a private or a public letter, to repel the attacks made upon his favourite character. Thus in a letter to a Russian lady[20] he says:

> "What, you too say that in drawing Bazarov I wished to make a caricature of the young generation. You repeat this—pardon my plain speaking—idiotic reproach. Bazarov, my favourite child, on whose account I quarrelled with Katkoff; Bazarov, on whom I lavished all the colours at my disposal; Bazarov, this man of intellect, this hero, a caricature! But I see it is useless for me to protest."

[20] *Souvenirs sur Tourguéneff*, 1887.

And in a letter addressed to the Russian students at Heidelberg he reiterates:

> "*Flatter comme un caniche*, I did not wish; although in this way I could no doubt have all the young men at once on my side; but I was unwilling to buy popularity by concessions of this kind. It is better to lose the campaign (and I believe I have lost it) than win by this subterfuge. I dreamed of a sombre, savage and great figure, only half emerged from barbarism, strong, *méchant* and honest, and nevertheless doomed to perish because it is always in advance of the future. I dreamed of a strange parallel to Pugatchev. And my young contemporaries shake their heads and tell me, '*Vous êtes foutu*, old fellow. You have insulted us. Your Arkady is far better. It's a pity you haven't worked him out a little more.' There is nothing left for me but, in the words of the gipsy song, 'to take off my hat with a very low bow.'"

What, then, is Bazarov?

Various writers have agreed in seeing in him only "criticism, pitiless, barren, and overwhelming analysis, and the spirit of absolute negation," but this is an error. Representing the creed which has produced the militant type of

Revolutionist in every capital of Europe, *he is the bare mind of Science first applied to Politics.* His own immediate origin is German Science interpreted by that spirit of logical intensity, Russian fanaticism, or devotion to the Idea, which is perhaps the distinguishing genius of the Slav. But he represents the roots of the modern Revolutionary movements in thought as well as in politics, rather than the branches springing from those roots. Inasmuch as the early work of the pure scientific spirit, knowing itself to be fettered by the superstitions, the confusions, the sentimentalities of the Past, was necessarily destructive, Bazarov's primary duty was to Destroy. In his essence, however, he stands for *the sceptical conscience of modern Science.* His watchword is *Reality*, and not Negation, as everybody in pious horror hastened to assert Turgenev, whose first and last advice to young writers was, "You need truth, remorseless truth, as regards your own sensations," was indeed moved to declare, "Except Bazarov's views on Art, I share almost all his convictions." The crude materialism of the 'sixties was not the basis of the scientific spirit, it was merely its passing expression; and the early Nihilists who denounced Art, the Family and Social Institutions were simply freeing themselves from traditions preparatory to a struggle that was inevitable. Again, though Bazarov is a Democrat, perhaps his kinship with the people is best proved by the contempt he feels for them. He stands forward essentially as an Individual, with the "isms" that can aid him, mere tools in his hand; Socialist, Communist or Individualist, in his necessary phases he fought this century against the tyranny of centralized Governments, and next century he will be fighting against the stupid tyranny of the Mass. Looking at Bazarov however, as a type that has played its part and vanished with its generation, as a man he is a new departure in history. His appearance marks the dividing-line between two religions, that of the Past—Faith, and that growing religion of to-day—Science. His is the duty of breaking away from all things that men call Sacred, and his savage egoism is essential to that duty. He is subject to neither Custom nor Law. He is his own law, and is occupied simply with the fact he is studying. He has thrown aside the ties of love and duty that cripple the advance of the strongest men. He typifies Mind grappling with Nature, seeking out her inexorable laws, Mind in pure devotion to the What Is, in startling contrast to the minds that follow their self-created kingdoms of What Appears and of What Ought to Be. He is therefore a foe to the poetry and art that help to increase Nature's glamour over man by alluring him to yield to her; for Bazarov's great aim is to see Nature at work behind the countless veils of illusions and ideals, and all the special functions of belief which she develops in the minds of the masses to get them unquestioning to do her bidding. Finally, Bazarov, in whom the comfortable compromising English mind sees only a man of bad form, bad taste, bad manners and overwhelming conceit, finally, Bazarov stands for Humanity awakened from century-old superstitions and the long dragging oppressive dream of tradition. Naked he stands under a deaf, indifferent sky, but he feels and knows that he has the strong brown earth beneath his feet.

This type, though it has developed into a network of special branches to-day, it is not difficult for us to trace as it has appeared and disappeared in the stormy periods of the last thirty years. Probably the genius and energy of the type was chiefly devoted to positive Science, and not to Politics; but it is sufficient to glance at the Revolutionary History, in theory and action, of the Continent to see that every movement was inspired by the ideas of the Bazarovs, though led by a variety of leaders. Just as the popular movements for Liberty fifty years earlier found sentimental and *romantic* expression in Byronism, so the popular movements of our time have been realistic in idea, and have looked to Science for their justification. Proudhon, Bakunin, Karl Marx, the Internationals, the Russian Terrorists, the Communists, all have a certain relation to Bazarov, but his nearest kinsmen in these and other movements we believe have worked, and have remained, obscure. It was a stroke of genius on Turgenev's part to make Bazarov die on the threshold unrecognized. He is Aggression, destroyed in his destroying. And there are many reasons in life for the Bazarovs remaining obscure. For one thing, their few disciples, the Arkadys, do not understand them; for another, the whole swarm of little interested persons who make up a movement are more or less engaged in personal interests, and they rarely take for a leader a man who works for his own set of truths, scornful of all cliques, penalties and rewards. Necessarily, too, the Bazarovs work alone, and are given the most dangerous tasks to accomplish unaided. Further, they are men whose brutal and breaking force attracts ten men where it repels a thousand. The average man is too afraid of Bazarov to come into contact with him. Again, the Bazarovs, as Iconoclasts, are always unpopular in their own circles. Yesterday in political life they were suppressed or exiled, and even in Science they were the men who were supplanted before their real claim was recognized, and to-day, when order reigns for a time, the academic circles and the popular critics will demonstrate that Bazarov's existence was a mistake, and the crowd could have got on much better without him.

The Crowd, the ungrateful Crowd! though for it Bazarov has wrested much from effete or corrupt hands, and has fought and weakened despotic and bureaucratic power, what has its opinion or memory to do with his brave heroic figure? Yes, heroic, as Turgenev, in indignation with Bazarov's shallow accusers, was betrayed into defining his own creation, Bazarov, whose very atmosphere is difficulty and danger, who cannot move without hostility carrying as he does destruction to the old worn-out truths, contemptuous of censure, still more contemptuous of praise, he goes his way against wind and tide. Brave man, given up to his cause, whatever it be, it is his joy *to stand alone*, watching the crowd as it races wherever reward is and danger is not. It is Bazarov's life to despise honours, success, opinion, and to let nothing, not love itself, come between him and his inevitable course, and, when death comes, to turn his face to the wall, while in the street below he can hear the voices of men cheering the popular hero who has last arrived. The Crowd! Bazarov is the antithesis of the cowardice of the Crowd. That is the secret why we love him.

III

As a piece of art *Fathers and Children* is the most powerful of all Turgenev's works. The figure of Bazarov is not only the political centre of the book, against which the other characters show up in their respective significance, but a figure in which the eternal tragedy of man's impotence and insignificance is realized in scenes of a most ironical human drama. How admirably this figure dominates everything and everybody. Everything falls away before this man's biting sincerity. In turn the figureheads of Culture and Birth, Nicolai and Pavel representing the Past; Arkady the sentimentalist representing the Present; the father and mother representing the ties of family that hinder a man's life-work; Madame Odintsov embodying the fascination of a beautiful woman—all fall into their respective places. But the particular power of *Fathers and Children*, of epic force almost, arises from the way in which Turgenev makes us feel the individual human tragedy of Bazarov in relation to the perpetual tragedy everywhere in indifferent Nature. In *On the Eve* Turgenev cast his figures against a poetic background by creating an atmosphere of War and Patriotism. But in *Fathers and Children* this poetic background is Nature herself, Nature who sows, with the same fling of her hand, life and death springing each from each, in the same rhythmical cast of fate. And with Nature for the background, there comes the wonderful sense conveyed to the reader throughout the novel, of the generations with their fresh vigorous blood passing away quickly, a sense of the coming generations, whose works, too, will be hurried away into the background, a sense of the silence of Earth, while her children disappear into the shadows, and are whelmed in turn by the inexorable night. While everything in the novel is expressed in the realistic terms of daily commonplace life, the characters appear now close to us as companions, and now they seem like distant figures walking under an immense sky; and the effect of Turgenev's simply and subtly drawn landscapes is to give us a glimpse of men and women in their actual relation to their mother earth and the sky over their heads. This effect is rarely conveyed in the modern Western novel, which deals so much with purely indoor life; but the Russian novelist gained artistic force for his tragedies by the vague sense ever present with him of the enormous distances of the vast steppes, bearing on their bosom the peasants' lives, which serve as a sombre background to the life of the isolated individual figures with which he is dealing. Turgenev has availed himself of this hidden note of tragedy, and with the greatest art he has made Bazarov, with all his ambition opening out before him, and his triumph awaited, the eternal type of man's conquering egoism conquered by the pin-prick of death. Bazarov, who looks neither to the right hand nor to the left, who delays no longer in his life-work of throwing off the mind-forged manacles; Bazarov, who trusts not to Nature, but would track the course of her most obscure laws; Bazarov, in his keen pursuit of knowledge, is laid low by the weapon he has selected to wield. His own tool, the dissecting knife, brings death to him, and his body is stretched beside the peasant who had gone before. Of the death scene, the great culmination of this great novel, it is impossible to speak without emotion. The voice of the reader, whosoever he be, must break when he comes to those passages of infinite pathos where the father, Vassily Ivanovitch, is seen peeping from behind the door at his dying son, where he cries, "Still living, my Yevgeny is still living, and now he will be saved. Wife, wife!" And where, when death has come, he cries, "I said I should rebel. I rebel, I rebel!" What art, what genius, we can only repeat, our spirit humbled to the dust by the exquisite solemnity of that undying simple scene of the old parents at the grave, the scene where Turgenev epitomizes in one stroke the infinite aspiration, the eternal insignificance of the life of man.

Let us end here with a repetition of a simple passage that, echoing through the last pages of *Fathers and Children*, must find an echo in the hearts of Turgenev's readers: "'To the memory of Bazarov,' Katya whispered in her husband's ear, ... but Arkady did not venture to propose the toast aloud." We, at all events, can drink the toast to-day as a poor tribute in recompense for those days when Turgenev in life proposed it, and his comrades looked on him with distrust, with coldness and with anger.

VIII
"SMOKE"

CHAPTER VIII

"SMOKE"

Smoke was first published in 1867, several years after Turgenev had fixed his home in Baden, with his friends the Viardots. Baden at this date was a favourite resort for all circles of Russian society, and Turgenev was able to study at his leisure his countrymen as they appeared to foreign critical eyes. The novel is therefore the most cosmopolitan of all Turgenev's works. On a veiled background of the great world of European society, little groups of representative Russians, members of the aristocratic and the Young Russia parties, are etched with an incisive, unfaltering hand. *Smoke*, as an historical study, though it yields in importance to *Fathers and Children* and *Virgin Soil*, is of great significance to Russians. It might with truth have been named *Transition*, for the generation it paints was then midway between the early philosophical Nihilism of the 'sixties and the active political Nihilism of the 'seventies.

Markedly transitional, however, as was the Russian mind of the days of *Smoke*, Turgenev, with the faculty that distinguishes the great artist from the artist of the second rank, the faculty of seeking out and stamping the essential under confused and fleeting forms, has once and for ever laid bare the fundamental weakness of the Slav nature, its weakness of will. *Smoke* is an attack, a deserved attack, not merely on the Young Russia party, but on all the Parties; not on the old ideas or the new ideas, but on the proneness of the Slav nature to fall a prey to a consuming weakness, a moral stagnation, a feverish *ennui*, the Slav nature that analyses everything with force and brilliancy, and ends, so often, by doing nothing. *Smoke* is the attack, bitter yet sympathetic, of a man who, with growing despair, has watched the weakness of his countrymen, while he loves his country all the more for the bitterness their sins have brought upon it. *Smoke* is the scourging of a babbling generation, by a man who, grown sick to death of the chatter of reformers and reactionists, is visiting the sins of the fathers on the children, with a contempt out of patience for the hereditary vice in the Slav blood. And this time the author cannot be accused of partisanship by any blunderer. "A plague o' both your houses" is his message equally to the Bureaucrats and the Revolutionists. And so skilfully does he wield the thong that every lash falls on the back of both parties. An exquisite piece of political satire is *Smoke*; for this reason alone it would stand unique among novels.

The attention that *Smoke* aroused was immediate and great; but the hue-and-cry that assailed it was even greater. The publication of the book marks the final rupture between Turgenev and the party of Young Russia. The younger generation never quite forgave him for drawing Gubaryov and Bambaev,

Voroshilov and Madame Suhantchikov—types, indeed, in which all revolutionary or unorthodox parties are painfully rich. Or, perhaps, Turgenev was forgiven for it when he was in his grave, a spot where forgiveness flowers to a late perfection. And yet the fault was not Turgenev's. No, his last novel, *Virgin Soil*, bears splendid witness that it was Young Russia that was one-eyed.

Let the plain truth here be set down. *Smoke* is not a complete picture of the Young Russia of the day; it was not yet time for that picture; and that being so, Turgenev did the next best thing in attacking the windbags, the charlatans and their crowd of shallow, chattering followers, as well as the empty formulas of the *laissez-faire* party. It was inevitable that the attack should bring on him the anger of all young enthusiasts working for "the Cause"; it was inevitable that "the Cause" of reform in Russia should be mixed up with the Gubaryovs, just as reforms in France a generation ago were mixed up with Boulanger; and that Turgenev's waning popularity for the last twenty years of his life should be directly caused by his honesty and clear-sightedness in regard to Russian Liberalism, was inevitable also. To be crucified by those you have benefited is the cross of honour of all great, single-hearted men.

But though the bitterness of political life flavours *Smoke*, although its points of departure and arrival are wrapped in the atmosphere of Russia's dark and insoluble problems, nevertheless the two central figures of the book, Litvinov and Irina, are not political figures. Luckily for them, in Gubaryov's words, they belong "to the undeveloped." Litvinov himself may be dismissed in a sentence. He is Turgenev's favourite type of man, a character much akin to his own nature, gentle, deep and sympathetic. Turgenev often drew such a character; Lavretsky, for example, in *A House of Gentlefolk*, is a first cousin to Litvinov, an older and a sadder man.

But Irina—Irina is unique; for Turgenev has in her perfected her type till she reaches a destroying witchery of fascination and subtlety. Irina will stand for ever in the long gallery of great creations, smiling with that enigmatical smile which took from Litvinov in a glance half his life, and his love for Tatyana. The special triumph of her creation is that she combines that exact balance between good and evil which makes good women seem insipid beside her and bad women unnatural. And, by nature irresistible, she is made doubly so to the imagination by the situation which she re-creates between Litvinov and herself. She ardently desires to become nobler, to possess all that the ideal of love means for the heart of woman; but she has only the power given to her of enervating the man she loves. Can she become a Tatyana to him? No, to no man. She is born to corrupt, yet never to be corrupted. She rises mistress of herself after the first measure of fatal delight. And, never giving her whole heart absolutely to her lover, she, nevertheless, remains ever to be desired.

Further, her wit, her scorn, her beauty preserve her from all the influences of evil she does not deliberately employ. Such a woman is as old and as rare a type as Helen of Troy. It is most often found among the mistresses of great princes, and it was from a mistress of Alexander II. that Turgenev modelled Irina.

Of the minor characters, Tatyana is an astonishing instance of Turgenev's skill in drawing a complete character with half a dozen strokes of the pen. The reader seems to have known her intimately all his life—her family life, her girlhood, her goodness and individual ways to the smallest detail; yet she only speaks on two or three occasions. Potugin is but a weary shadow of Litvinov, but it is difficult to say how much this is a telling refinement of art. The shadow of this prematurely exhausted man is cast beforehand by Irina across Litvinov's future. For Turgenev to have drawn Potugin as an ordinary individual would have vulgarized the novel and robbed it of its skilful proportions, for Potugin is one of those shadowy figures which supply the chiaroscuro to a brilliant etching.

As a triumphant example of consummate technical skill, *Smoke* will repay the most exact scrutiny. There are a lightness and a grace about the novel that conceal its actual strength. The political argument glides with such ease in and out of the love story, that the hostile critic is absolutely baffled; and while the most intricate steps are executed in the face of a crowd of angry enemies, the performer lands smiling and in safety. The art by which Irina's disastrous fascination results in falsity, and Litvinov's desperate striving after sincerity ends in rehabilitation—the art by which these two threads are spun, till their meaning colours the faint political message of the book, is so delicate that, like the silken webs which gleam only for the first fresh hours in the forest, it leaves no trace, but becomes a dream in the memory. And yet this book, which has the freshness of windy rain and the whirling of autumn leaves, is the story of disintegrating weakness, of the passion that saps and paralyses, that renders life despicable, as Turgenev himself says. *Smoke* is the finest example in literature of a subjective psychological study of passion rendered clearly and objectively in terms of art. Its character—we will not say its superiority—lies in the extraordinary clearness with which the most obscure mental phenomena are analysed in relation to the ordinary values of daily life. At the precise point of psychological analysis where Tolstoy wanders and does not convince the reader, and at the precise point where Dostoevsky's analysis seems exaggerated and obscure, like a figure looming through the mist, Turgenev throws a ray of light from the outer to the inner world of man, and the two worlds are revealed in the natural depths of their connection. It is in fact difficult to find among the great modern artists men whose natural balance of intellect can be said to equalize their special genius. The Greeks alone present to the world a spectacle of a triumphant harmony in the critical and creative mind of man, and this is their great pre-eminence. But *Smoke* presents the curious feature of a novel (Slav in virtue of its modern psychological genius) which is classical in its treatment and expression throughout; the balance of Turgenev's intellect reigns ever supreme over the natural morbidity of his subject.

IX
"VIRGIN SOIL"

CHAPTER IX

"VIRGIN SOIL"

The last words of *Virgin Soil*—

> "A long while Paklin remained standing before this closed door.
>
> "'Anonymous Russia!' he said at last"—

lay bare the inner meaning of the book. Anonymous Russia! It was Anonymous Russia, as Turgenev saw, that had at last arisen to menace the doors which shut out Russia from political liberty. And it is of the spontaneous formation of the Nihilist party, and of the hurried and uncertain steps it took preparatory to the serious Terrorist struggle, that *Virgin Soil* treats with equal skill and force. The educated young Russian of the 'seventies had begun to live an underground life; Turgenev studied this phenomenon, and, difficult though this study was, so well did he foresee the future of Young Russia that *Virgin Soil* remains the best analysis made of the national elements that were mingled in its loosely-knit secret organizations. *Virgin Soil* gives us the historical justification of the Nihilist movement, and the prophecy of its surface failure; it traces out the deep roots of the necessity of such a movement; it shows forth the ironical and inevitable weakness of this party of self-sacrifice. This effect is obtained in this novel by a series of significant suggestions underlying the words and actions of the characters.

These suggestions are delicate and fleeting like the quiet swirl of water round the sunken rocks in a stream. And so delicately is the Nihilist rising shadowed forth, that a foreign reader can enjoy the novel simply for its human, and not for its political, interest. Delicate, however, as is the technique of *Virgin Soil*, there is a large, free carelessness in the spirit of its art which reminds one much of the few last plays of Shakespeare, notably of *Cymbeline*, where the action, so easygoing is it, is almost too natural and effortless to be called *art*. In reality this large carelessness is a sign that the stage of the artist's maturity has been reached, and a little passed. *Virgin Soil*, one must admit, is artistically the least perfect of the six great novels. The opening is too leisurely, and not till the second volume is reached do we feel that Turgenev is exerting his full power over us. The characterization is less subtle in detail. While Markelov's figure is somewhat enigmatic, Paklin, though extremely life-like, too obviously serves the purpose of a go-between. But if people declare that Kallomyetsev is a type caricatured, we protest that the portrait of Sipyagin, this statesman of "the most liberal opinions," is priceless. The scene between Sipyagin and Paklin in chapter xxxiv., especially the portion in the carriage, is psychologically a gem of the first water. *Virgin Soil* was the last of

Turgenev's great novels, and appropriately ends his career as novelist; it was his last word to the young; it was one of the causes of his final disgrace with the Government; it was his link with most of Russia's great writers: they were exiled in life: Turgenev was exiled after death. After his funeral at Petersburg, September 1883, attended by 285 deputations, public comments on his labours were discreetly veiled and discreetly suppressed by the Government,[21] that had feared his power in life. And this fatuous act of the autocracy is the best commentary on the truth of *Virgin Soil*.

[21] For an account of the suppression and prohibition of Tolstoy's lecture on Turgenev, in Moscow, after the latter's death, see Maude's *Life of Tolstoy*, vol. ii, p. 185.

To examine the characters of the novel is to see how representative they were of Russian political life. Nezhdanov, the poet and half-aristocrat, is one of the most important. Turgenev makes him the child of a *mésalliance*, and he is, in fact, the bastard child of Power allied to modern Sentimentality. Born with the brain of an aristocrat, he represents the uneasy educated conscience of the aristocrats, the conscience which is ever seeking to propitiate, and be responsible for, "the people," but is ever driven back by its inability to make itself understood by the masses, which have been crystallized by hard facts, for hundreds of years, into a great caste of their own. Nezhdanov understands instinctively how impossible, how fatal, is the task of "going to the people": his sympathy is with them, but not of them. Banished, by his attitude, from his own caste, he seeks refuge in poetry and art; but there is not enough of reality, not enough of the national life, in his art for him to feel himself more than a dilettante. He feels he must identify himself with the real movements around him, or perish. He fails in his impossible task of winning over "the people," and perishes. The Nezhdanovs still exist in Europe: they are the sign of a dislocation of the national life and of the artificial conditions of the society in which they appear; and the Russian Nezhdanov of the 'seventies was a type very much in evidence in the Nihilist party, and by making his hero perish Turgenev wished to show that hope for the future lay with far different men—with the Mariannas, the moral enthusiasts, and with the Solomins, the practical leaders who must come from "the people" itself.

In drawing Nezhdanov, Turgenev was on his own ground: the type was very sympathetic to him, for he too felt all his life with despair that the gulf that separated "the people" from those who would lead them, was too great to be successfully crossed; and his own inner life was a turning away from the politicians, who traduced him and watched him with suspicion, to art as a refuge from reality. But in drawing Solomin, the leader coming from the people, Turgenev did not achieve perfect artistic success. The truth is, this type was then a scarce one, and to-day it is not prominent. It is this type of man that Russia needs more than any other, the man of firmness and *character*. Solomin is admirably drawn in the amusing scene of his visit to the Sipyagins (chaps. xxiii.-xxv.); also in his relations with Nezhdanov and Marianna, as their host at the factory; but there is a slight veil drawn over his inner life, and he is never sounded to the depths. Does he present enough of the rich contradictions and human variations of a living man? True, Solomin typifies the splendid sturdiness of the Russian people, the caution and craftiness of the peasant-born and the intellectual honesty of his race; but perhaps these qualities need a more individual soul behind them to combine them into a perfect creation. And in fact the Russian Solomins have not yet left the factories: they are the foremen who do not speak up enough for "the people" in the national life.[22]

[22] Passage written in 1896.

Marianna, however, the young girl, the Nihilist enthusiast, is the success of the book. The splendid qualities shown by the Nihilist women in the Terrorist campaign, a few years later than the publication of *Virgin Soil*, are a striking testimony to Turgenev's genius in psychology. The women of Young Russia were waiting to be used, and used the women were. Marianna is the incarnation of that Russian fight for progress, which, though half-hidden and obscure to foreign eyes, has thrilled the nerves of Europe. This pure girl with passionate, courageous soul is, in fact, the Liberty of Russia. Without experience or help, with eyes bandaged by her destiny, she calmly goes forward on the far journey whence there is no return. By necessity she must go on: she lives by faith. In her figure is personified the flower of the Russian youth, those who cast off from their generation the stigma of inaction—that heart-eating inaction which is the vice of the Russian temperament, as her great writers tell us—those who cast fear to the Sipyagins, and the Kallomyetsevs, to the bureaucrats their enemies, and went forth on that campaign, sublime in its recklessness, fruitful in its consequences to their country and fatal in its consequences to themselves. Marianna personifies the spirit of self-sacrifice which led her comrades forth against autocracy. The path was closed; behind them was only dishonour and cowardice; onward, then, for honour, for liberty, for all that makes life worth living to the courageous in heart. But the closed doors, the doors on which they knocked, were the doors of the fortress: the fortress closed upon them, upon their brothers and sisters: their leaders were sentenced, deported, exiled: fresh leaders sprang up, each circle had its leaders, whose average life, as free men, was reckoned, not by years but by months. The lives of Marianna and her generation were spent in prison or in exile. But by the very recklessness of their protest against autocracy, by their very simplicity in "going to the people," by their self-immolation for their principles Europe knew that there was no liberty in Russia save in its prisons, and that the bloody reprisals that followed were those of Marianna's brothers, who saw her helpless in the hands of a great gendarmerie—a gendarmerie that had long shamelessly abused the power it held, that had silenced brutally all who had protested, all, all the independent spirits, all their great writers, all their *men*. Marianna, Marianna herself, must seek the prison! Turgenev foresaw this, and *Virgin Soil* tells of her preparation for the ordeal, of the why and the wherefore she went on her path.

And if anything remains obscure in *Virgin Soil*, the English reader must remember that Turgenev was writing under special difficulties. There must always be a little vagueness in one's speech, when *Silence* is written in an official writing above the doors. Anonymous Russia! Anonymous Russia had arisen to mine the doors: the doors must be shattered by secret hands that Europe might for once gaze through. It was for Turgenev's breaking of this *Silence* that Tolstoy was forbidden to speak when Turgenev had been carried to his tomb. It was for Marianna's transgression against this *Silence* that Turgenev has glorified her in *Virgin Soil*.

What was the Nihilist party of the 'seventies? It began, as we have said, with the Socialistic movement of "going to the people." This movement, again, was the natural outlet for the many liberal ideas which, germinating in "advanced" heads, had been gathering in intensity with each generation. With the liberation of the serfs Alexander II.'s liberal policy had abruptly ended. To understand Russian politics is to know that though there are many cliques there are only two great parties, the one orthodox, the other unorthodox—the party of Governmental Action, and the party of Liberal Ideas. There are no safe politics in Russia outside the official world. If you can win over the officials to your plans in various local work, well and good; if not, your efforts are labelled "subversive"; and it is thus that, sooner or later, every disciple of liberal ideas finds himself placed in direct opposition to the Government. Though there are many liberal-minded men among the officials, still, in Solomin's words, "the official is always an outsider," and therefore it is that the unofficial thinking part of Russia—the writers, the professors, the students, the press, and the more intelligent of the professional world—form an unorganized but permanent opposition. To this party gravitate naturally the discontented spirits from all classes—nobles, military men, those who have been hardly dealt with, and those who have an axe of their own to grind—the Markelovs, and the Paklins. Accordingly, the autocracy, by the solid, impermeable front it has presented for twenty-five years to reform and to the education of the peasants, may be said to hold the varying opposition together. The action of the Government, too, in forbidding the public to comment on such matters as the late strike of factory hands in Petersburg, where also the masters were "forbidden" to yield to the men's demands, constantly creates a hostile public. And it was in this manner that the Nihilist party of the 'seventies was formed.

It was natural enough for the last generation of Young Russia "to go to the people," for it is in the matter of the education of the peasants that Russia's hope of social and political reform lies. Besides, this plan of action meant for Young Russia the taking of the path of least resistance. The other paths had been closed by reactionary decrees. But to go actually among the peasantry and work for them and learn from them had never been attempted, and by a natural impulse the Young Russia theorists threw themselves into this Utopian campaign. The movement, of course, was fore-doomed. Not only did the Government enact harsh penalties against the Socialists, but the peasants themselves were too ignorant, too far off in their life, to understand what Young Russia meant. And the exiling and imprisonment of the leading propagandists, when it came, could not fail to bring the Nihilists into a direct war with autocracy itself.

The whole quarrel between the autocracy and the liberal opposition, a quarrel which the Nihilists of the late 'seventies brought to a head, is a question of liberty. Is Russia to be more Orientalized or more Europeanized? If you believe in liberty of speech and of the conscience, in a free press and the education of the peasants, if you would reform the peculation and corruption of the official world, if you wish to circulate European literature without hindrance, if you detest the persecution of the Jews and the Stundists,—then you must be silent or be prepared at any moment for bureaucratic warnings, deprivations, detentions and possible exile. If you are a Conservative you will acquiesce in every possible action of the bureaucracy, as "necessary." It is simply a struggle between a very strongly organized bureaucracy, armed with the modern weapons of centralized power, and the public opinion of a large body of educated subjects with advanced views. Though enormous power is in the hands of the Government, and the gross credulity and ignorance of the peasants and the self-interest of the officials all work to preserve the *status quo*, nevertheless there is in the Russian mind, side by side with its natural Slavophilism, a great susceptibility to European example, and therefore the work of the Nihilists of yesterday and the Liberals of to-day was, and is, *to awaken the public mind*. It does not matter very much how this work is performed, so long as it is performed. The Russian mind is naturally quick and sensitive; it moves quickly to conclusions when once it is started, as we see in the quickness with which Russia was semi-Europeanized by Peter the Great, and how easily the Emancipation of the Serfs was effected owing to the weakness of the autocracy at the close of the Crimean War. There is reaction now in Russia, but this may be broken up by the pressure of a series of fresh economic difficulties superimposed upon the old.

It can only, therefore, be claimed for the Nihilists of the 'seventies that they represented an advanced section of the community, and not the nation itself, in their struggle with the bureaucracy. They must be regarded as enthusiasts who awoke public opinion when it had begun to slumber. They vindicated the manliness of the nation, which had always gone in fear of the official world: it was now the bureaucracy that was afraid! The Nihilists became martyrs for their creed of progress; they drew the attention of Europe to the strange spectacle that Russia presents in its well-equipped bureaucracy of caste slowly paralysing the old democratic institutions of the peasantry. A strong Governmental system is absolutely necessary for the holding together of the enormous Russian Empire; but the fact that the work of freeing and educating the peasants had (with only the rarest exceptions), been always violently or secretly opposed by the high officials, suggests that the bureaucracy is like a parasite which strangles, though appearing to protect, the tree itself. And the attitude of the official world to its sun and centre, the autocracy, is something like that of threatening soldiers surrounding the throne of a latter-day Caesarism.

Whether or no the Nihilists' belief in revolution in Russia was justified by their measure of success, their rising was but a long-threatened revolt of idealism and of the Russian conscience against Russian cowardice; it was the fermentation of modern ideas in the breast of a society iron-bound by officialism; it was the generous aspiration of the Russian soul against sloth and apathy and greed. The Nihilists failed, inasmuch as the battle of Liberty is yet to be won: they succeeded, inasmuch as their revolt was a tremendous object-lesson to Europe of the internal evils of their country. And the objection that they borrowed their ideas of revolution from the Commune and were not a genuine product of Russia, Turgenev has answered once for all in *Virgin Soil*. Liberty must spring from the soil whence Marianna springs.

In the words of that great poem of Whitman:

> "The battle rages with many a loud alarm and frequent advance and retreat,
>
> The infidel triumphs, or supposes he triumphs,
>
> The prison, scaffold, garotte, hand-cuffs, iron necklace, and lead balls do their work,
>
> The named and unnamed heroes pass to other spheres,
>
> The great speakers and writers are exiled, they lie sick in distant lands,
>
> The cause is asleep, the strongest throats are choked with their own blood.

The young men droop their eyelashes towards the ground when they meet.

But for all this Liberty has not gone out of the place, nor the infidel entered into full possession,

When Liberty goes out of the place it is not the first to go, nor the second or third to go,

It waits for all the rest to go, it is the last."

There is no going back for the Mariannas of Russia. They must go forward, and to-day they are going forward. Honour to them and theirs, to them who, if forbidden by authority to work in the light, are ready again to work in the dark. Honour to that great party with whom their country's liberties have remained—Anonymous Russia!

Much water has flowed under the bridge since the preface above was written one-and-twenty years ago, but the author has only deemed it necessary to correct a few lines of his criticism and to modify his statement concerning Turgenev's funeral. Since 1896, we have seen the spectacle of the Russo-Japanese war, the General Strike, the creation of the Duma, the abortive Revolution of 1905, the excesses of Terrorists, Agent-Provocateurs, "Black Hundreds" and Military Court-Martials, Governmental illegalities, the rapid evolution, economic and political, of a new Russia till 1914; and finally the spectacle of the Great European War, the rally of all parties, under the Prussian invasion, to the patriotic programme of the Progressive Bloc, the falling away of even the old-fashioned Bureaucrats from "the dark forces of the Empire," and the general situation, in the words of the *Times* Petrograd correspondent:

> "A DELAYED DEVELOPMENT
>
> "We know that had the Constitution signed by Alexander II. been introduced, Russia might have been spared much suffering. The assassination of the Tsar brought about a delay of 25 precious years. Pobiedonostzeff persuaded Alexander III. that Russia enjoyed a special dispensation of Providence; that the laws of history in other lands did not apply to her. Thus the greatest of reforms, introduced in the 'sixties, the abolition of slavery and the institution of the Zemstvos granting the people a voice in the affairs of their country, became stultified. It is true that serfdom could not be reintroduced, that Zemstvos could not be abolished, but what happened was bad enough. The education of the

masses was neglected and the local assemblies were placed under tutelage.

"Not till 1905 did Russia obtain relief from the reaction that followed upon the tragedy of 1881. But Pobiedonostzeff had numerous adherents among his contemporaries in the older bureaucracy, many of whom survive to this day. The governing class in Russia forms a caste which directs a huge and highly intricate mechanism of a centralized administration ruling nearly 200,000,000 of people. These statesmen could not suddenly be eliminated or instilled with new ideas alien to all their habits or traditions. In the Senate or Supreme Court of Justice, which promulgates all laws and sees to their enforcement, and in the Upper House, which is half composed of members appointed from the ranks of these elder statesmen, the old leaven was still unhappily strong.... To these causes and agencies we owe the reaction that has characterized Russian internal politics within recent years....

"Slowly but surely the ranks of the old reactionary party have been declining. By an infallible process of attrition they were bound to disappear sooner or later, leaving the field clear for the New Russia. The Great War came before the elimination was consummated. It has hastened the process by convincing everybody, including the bureaucracy, of the utter failure of the old system to cope with great national problems. At the present time no section of the population, and, therefore, no genuine political party, exists in Russia that has a word to say in support of the Pobiedonostzeff theory. The Nobles' Congress was the last stronghold to surrender. It did so in the most emphatic manner by endorsing, *mirabile dictu!* the resolutions of both Houses of Parliament demanding the formation of a strong, united Ministry enjoying the confidence of the people. Between the Army and the nation there is not, and there cannot be, any difference of opinion on this subject.

"Within something like ten years the Russian people have become a new people. What Pobiedonostzeff succeeded in doing 25 years ago cannot, obviously, be attempted now. Russia has finally, irrevocably, turned her back upon the old ideas. She has spoken her mind fully, unanimously."—*The Times*, February 8, 1917.

As the writer is retouching his last chapter comes the news of the Russian Revolution, an event of no less import to Europe than was the French Revolution, and one no less fraught with incalculable consequences.

This event carries back one's thought to the revolutionary attempt of the Decembrists, 1825, and to the successive movements for political reform in Turgenev's own day, from the men of the "'forties" (*Rudin*) to the disastrous obscurantism of the heavy, stupid-minded Alexander III., and his reactionary ministers. From *Virgin Soil*, 1877, one follows in thought the succeeding forty years in which tract after tract of stubborn political virgin soil has been slowly broken up and sown with progressive seed. The changing economic conditions, aggravated by the Great European War, and the weak obstinacy of Nicholas II. have, at last, bankrupted the Autocracy.

The result signally vindicates Turgenev's political prescience and his *rôle* as the interpreter of Western culture and Western liberalism to his countrymen. For until the great barrier of petrified Bureaucratic Nationalism was broken down, true democratic Nationalism could not flow in free channels. Slavophilism, with its leading idea of the deliverance of Europe by the Autocracy, by Orthodoxy and the communal love of the meek Russian peasant, must be replaced by a new movement, spiritual in its essence, and give much-needed fresh conceptions to our materialized Western civilization. Every reader of Russian literature, from Gogol to our day, cannot fail to recognize that the Russian mind is superior to the English in its emotional breadth and flexibility, its eager responsiveness to new ideas, its spontaneous warmth of nature. With all their faults the Russian people are more permeated with humane love and living tenderness, in their social practice, than those of other nations. Let us trust that the Russian earth, no longer clouded by a dark, overcast sky, will be flooded with the fertilizing sunlight of this new, democratic Nationalism.

Turgenev stood, in the 'seventies, between the camps of the extremists, the old nobility who worked to prevent, hinder or suppress every reform, and the shallow, hot-headed theorists, who wished to force the pace, but whose talk ended in "smoke." Consequently he was frequently accused of cowardice by the revolutionaries on the one hand, and by the Conservatives of complicity with the revolutionaries, on the other.[23] As *an artist*, while he stood aside from direct political action, his attitude to the revolutionaries appeared necessarily ambiguous. Pavlovsky, however, has well characterized it:

> "We see therefore that Turgenev was too variable to be in any sense a man of politics. He was never a Nihilist nor a Revolutionary, and those episodes we have cited are advanced only to show he considered the revolutionaries as

an artist. As such they excited his imagination and carried him away like a child. Immediately after reflection he became sceptical and—this was his ordinary mental disposition—never believing in solid results of these agitators, though he retained always great sympathy for the Youth, whom he esteemed beyond all for their constant spirit of self-sacrifice. Both these mental tendencies are clearly to be seen in two of his *Poems in Prose*, 'The Workman and the Man with White Hands,' and 'The Threshold!'"

[23] See the letter to Madame Viardot, of January 19, 1864, in which Turgenev describes how he was summoned before a Tribunal of the Senate to answer charges of plotting with the revolutionaries, which he did without any trouble.

In Paris, in his last years, Turgenev was in active touch with the colony of young Russians, and assisted with his purse and his advice a number of protégés. A ridiculous hubbub arose in the Russian press on the publication in the *Temps* of Turgenev's preface to *En Cellule*, a tale by one of these protégés, Pavlovsky, and Turgenev in a letter to the *Malva* thereupon defined his political faith:

"PARIS, *December 30, 1879.*

"Without vanity or circumlocution, and merely stating facts I have the right to say that my convictions put on record in the press and in other sources, have not changed an iota in the last forty years. I have never hidden them from any one. To the young I have always been and have remained a moderate, a liberal of the old-fashioned stamp, a man who looks for reforms from above, and is opposed to the revolution.

"If young Russia appreciated me it was in that light, and if the ovations offered were dear to me, it was precisely because I did not go to seek the young generation, but it who came to me."

Turgenev's political creed may be read without the slightest ambiguity between the lines of *A Sportsman's Sketches* and his great novels. It is a creed of the necessity of the people's mental and spiritual enlightenment, of the amelioration of bad social conditions and of the establishment of constitutional government, in the place of despotism.[24]

[24] Kropotkin tells us: "I saw Turgenev for the last time in the autumn of 1881. He was very ill, and worried by the thought that it was his duty to write to Alexander III. who had just come to the throne, and hesitated as to the

policy he should follow—asking him to give Russia a constitution, and proving to him by solid arguments the necessity of that step. With evident grief he said to me, 'I feel that I must do it, but I feel I shall not be able to do it.' In fact, he was already suffering awful pains occasioned by a cancer in the spinal cord, and had the greatest difficulty in sitting up and talking for a few moments. He did not write then, and a few weeks later it would have been useless, Alexander III. had announced in a manifesto his resolution to remain the absolute ruler of Russia."—*Memoirs of a Revolutionist*, vol. ii. p. 222.

X
THE TALES

CHAPTER X

THE TALES

In addition to his six great novels Turgenev published, between 1846 and his death in 1883, about forty tales which reflect as intimately social atmospheres of the 'thirties, 'forties and 'fifties as do Tchehov's stories atmospheres of the 'eighties and 'nineties. Several of these tales, as *The Torrents of Spring*, are of considerable length, but their comparatively simple structure places them definitely in the class of the *conte*. While their form is generally free and straightforward, the narrative, put often in the mouth of a character who by his comments and asides exchanges at will his active rôle for that of a spectator, is capable of the most subtle modulations. An examination of the chronological order of the tales shows how very delicately Turgenev's art is poised between realism and romanticism. In his finest examples, such as *The Brigadier* and *A Lear of the Steppes*, the two elements fuse perfectly, like the meeting of wave and wind in sea foam. "Nature placed Turgenev between poetry and prose," says Henry James; and if one hazards a definition we should prefer to term Turgenev *a poetic realist*.

In our first chapter we glanced at *The Duellist*, and in the same year (1846) appeared *The Jew*, a close study, based on a family anecdote, of Semitic double-dealing and family feeling: also *Three Portraits*, a more or less faithful ancestral chronicle. This latter tale, though the hero is of the proud, bad, "Satanic" order of the romantic school, is firmly objective, as is also *Pyetushkov* (1847), whose lively, instinctive realism is so bold and intimate as to contradict the compliment that the French have paid themselves—that Turgenev ever had need to dress his art by the aid of French mirrors.

Although *Pyetushkov* shows us, by a certain open *naïveté* of style, that a youthful hand is at work, it is the hand of a young master carrying out Gogol's satiric realism with finer point, to find a perfect equilibrium free from bias or caricature. The essential strength of the realistic method is developed in *Pyetushkov* to its just limits, and note it is the Russian realism carrying the warmth of life into the written page, which warmth the French so often lose in clarifying their impressions and crystallizing them in art. Observe how the reader is transported bodily into Pyetushkov's stuffy room, how the Major fairly boils out of the two pages he lives in, and how Onisim and Vassilissa and the aunt walk and chatter around the stupid Pyetushkov, and laugh at him behind his back in a manner that exhales the vulgar warmth of these people's lower-class world. One sees that the latter holds few secrets for Turgenev. Three years earlier had appeared *Andrei Kolosov* (1844), a sincere diagnosis of youth's sentimental expectations, raptures and remorse, in presence of the other sex, in this case a girl who is eager for a suitor. The sketch is characteristically Russian in its analytic honesty, but Turgenev's charm is here lessened by his over-literal exactitude. And passing to *The Diary of a Superfluous Man* (1850), we must remark that this famous study of a type of a petty provincial Hamlet reveals a streak of suffused sentimentalism in Turgenev's nature, one which comes to the surface the more subjective is the handling of his theme, and the less his great technical skill in *modelling* his subject is called for. The last-named story belongs to a group with which we must place *Faust* (1853), *Yakov Pasinkov* (1855), *A Correspondence* (1855) and even the tender and charming *Acia* (1857), all of which stories, though rich in emotional shades and in beautiful descriptions, are lacking in fine chiselling. The melancholy yearning of the heroes and heroines through failure or misunderstanding, though no doubt true to life, seems to-day too imbued with emotional hues of the Byronic romanticism of the period, and in this small group of stories Turgenev's art is seen definitely dated, even old-fashioned.

In *The Country Inn* (1852), we are back on the firm ground of an objective study of village types, with clear, precise outlines, a detailed drawing from nature, strong yet subtle; as is also *Mumu* (1852), one based on a household episode that passed before Turgenev's youthful eyes, in which the deaf-mute Gerassim, a house serf, is defrauded first of the girl he loves, and then of his little dog, Mumu, whom he is forced to drown, stifling his pent-up affection, at the caprice of his tyrannical old mistress. The story is a classic example of Turgenev's tender insight and beauty of feeling. As delicate, but more varied in execution is *The Backwater*, with its fresh, charming picture of youth's *insouciance* and readiness to take a wrong turning, a story which in its atmospheric freshness and emotional colouring may be compared with Tchehov's studies of youth in *The Seagull*, a play in which the neurotic spiritual descendants of Marie and Nadejda, Veretieff and Steltchinsky, appear and pass into the shadows. This note of the fleetingness of youth and happiness reappears in *A Tour of the Forest* (1857), where Turgenev's acute sense of man's ephemeral life in face of the eternity of nature finds full expression. The description, here, of the vast, gloomy, murmuring pine forest, with its cold, dim solitudes, is finely contrasted with the passing outlook of the peasants, Yegor, Kondrat, and the wild Efrem. (See p. 16.)

The rich colour and perfume of Turgenev's delineation of romantic passion are disclosed when we turn to *First Love* (1860), which details the fervent adoration of Woldemar, a boy of sixteen, for the fascinating Zinaïda, an exquisite creation, who, by her mutability and caressing, mocking caprice keeps her bevy of eager suitors in suspense till at length she yields herself in her passion to Woldemar's father. This study of the intoxication of adolescent love is, again, based on an episode of Turgenev's youth, in which he and his father played the identical rôles of Woldemar and his father. Here we tremble on the magic borderline between prose and poetry, and the fragrance of blossoming love instincts is felt pervading all the fluctuating impulses of grief, tenderness, pity and regret which combine in the tragic close. The profoundly haunting apostrophe to youth is indeed a pure lyric. Passing to *Phantoms* (1863), which we discuss with *Prose Poems* (see p. 200), the truth of Turgenev's confession that spiritually and sensuously he was saturated with the love of woman and ever inspired by it, is confirmed. In his description of Alice, the winged phantom-woman, who gradually casts her spell over the sick hero, luring him to fly with her night after night over the vast expanse of earth, Turgenev has in a mysterious manner, all his own, concentrated the very essence of woman's possessive love. Alice's hungry yearning for self-completion, her pleading arts, her sad submissiveness, her rapture in her hesitating lover's embrace, are artistically a sublimation of all the impressions and instincts by which woman fascinates, and fulfils her purpose of creation. The projection of this shadowy woman's love-hunger on the mighty screen of the night earth, and the merging of her power in men's restless energies, felt and divined through the sweeping tides of nature's incalculable forces, is an inspiration which, in its lesser fashion, invites comparison with Shakespeare's creative vision of nature and the supernatural.

In his treatment of the supernatural Turgenev, however, sometimes missed his mark. *The Dog* (1866) is of a coarser and indeed of an ordinary texture. With the latter story may be classed *The Dream* (1876), curiously Byronic in imagery and atmosphere, and artistically not convincing. Far more sincere, psychologically, is *Clara Militch* (1882), a penetrating study of a passionate temperament, a story based on a tragedy of Parisian life. In our opinion *The Song of Triumphant Love*, though exquisite in its jewelled mediaeval details, has been overrated by the French, and Turgenev's genius is here seen contorted and cramped by the *genre*.

To return to the tales of the 'sixties. *Lieutenant Yergunov's Story*, though its strange atmosphere is cunningly painted, is not of the highest quality, comparing unfavourably with *The Brigadier* (1867), the story of the ruined nobleman, Vassily Guskov, with its tender, sub-ironical studies of odd characters, Narkiz and Cucumber. *The Brigadier* has a peculiarly fascinating poignancy, and must be prized as one of the rarest of Turgenev's high achievements, even as the connoisseur prizes the original beauty of a fine Meryon etching. The tale is a microcosm of Turgenev's own nature; his love of Nature, his sympathy with all humble, ragged, eccentric, despised human creatures, his unfaltering, keen gaze into character, his perfect eye for relative values in life, all mingle in *The Brigadier* to create for us a sense of the vicissitudes of life, of how a generation of human seed springs and flourishes awhile on earth and soon withers away under the menacing gaze of the advancing years.

A complete contrast to *The Brigadier* is the sombre and savagely tragic piece of realism, *An Unhappy Girl* (1868). As a study of a coarse and rapacious nature the portrait of Mr. Ratsch, the Germanized Czech, is a revelation of the depths of human swinishness. Coarse malignancy is here "the power of darkness" which closes, as with a vice, round the figure of the proud, helpless, exquisite girl, Susanna. There is, alas, no exaggeration in this unrelenting, painful story. The scene of Susanna's playing of the Beethoven sonata (chapter xiii.) demonstrates how there can be no truce between a vile animal nature and pure and beautiful instincts, and a faint suggestion symbolic of the national "dark forces" at work in Russian history deepens the impression. The worldly power of greed, lust and envy, ravaging, whether in war or peace, which seize on the defenceless and innocent, as their prey, here triumphs over Susanna, the victim of Mr. Ratsch's violence. The last chapter, the banquet scene, satirizes "the dark forest" of the heart when greed and baseness find their allies in the inertness, sloth or indifference of the ordinary man.

A Strange Story (1869) has special psychological interest for the English mind in that it gives clues to some fundamental distinctions between the Russian and the Western soul. Sophie's words, "You spoke of the will—that's what must be broken," seems strange to English thought. To be lowly, to be suffering, despised, to *be* unworthy, this desire implies that the Slav character is apt to be lacking in *will*, that it finds it easier to resign itself than to make the effort to be triumphant or powerful. The Russian people's attitude, historically, may, indeed, be compared to a bowl which catches and sustains what life brings it; and the Western people's to a bowl inverted to ward off what fate drops from the impassive skies. The mental attitude of the Russian peasant indeed implies that in blood he is nearer akin to the Asiatics than the Russian ethnologists wish to allow. Certainly in the inner life, intellectually, morally and emotionally, the Russian is a half-way house between the Western and Eastern races, just as geographically he spreads over the two continents.

Brilliant also is *Knock-Knock-Knock* (1870), a psychological study, of "a man fated," a Byronic type of hero, dear to the heart of the writers of the romantic period. Sub-Lieutenant Teglev, the melancholy, self-centred hero, whose prepossession of a tragic end nothing can shake, so that he ends by throwing himself into the arms of death, this portrait is most cunningly fortified by the wonderfully life-like atmosphere of the river fog in which the suicide is consummated. Turgenev's range of mood is disclosed in *Punin and Baburin* (1874), a leisurely reminiscence of his mother's household; but the delicious blending of irony and kindness in the treatment of both Punin and Baburin atones for the lengthy conclusion. Of *The Watch* (1875), a story for boys, nothing here need be said, except that it is inferior to the delightful *The Quail*, a *souvenir d'enfance* written at the Countess Tolstoy's request for an audience of children. In considering *A Lear of the Steppes* (1870), *The Torrents of Spring* (1871) and *A Living Relic* (1874), we shall sum up here our brief survey of Turgenev's achievement in the field of the *conte*.

In *The Torrents of Spring* the charm, the grace, the power of Turgenev's vision are seen bathing his subject, revealing all its delicate lineaments in a light as fresh and tender as that of a day of April sunlight in Italy. *Torrents* of Spring, not Spring Floods, be it remarked, is the true significance of the Russian, telling of a moment of the year when all the forces of Nature are leaping forth impetuously, the mounting sap, the hill streams, the mating birds, the blood in the veins of youth. The opening perhaps is a little over-leisurely, this description of the Italian confectioner's family, and its fortunes in Frankfort, but how delightful is the contrast in racial spirit between the pedantic German shop-manager, Herr Klüber and Pantaleone, and the lovely Gemma. But the long opening prelude serves as a foil to heighten the significant story of the seduction of the youthful Sanin by Maria Nikolaevna, that clear-eyed "huntress of men"; one of the most triumphant feminine portraits in the whole range of fiction. The spectator feels that this woman in her ruthless charm is the incarnation of a cruel principle in Nature, while we watch her preparing to strike her talons into her fascinated, struggling prey. Her spirit's essence, in all its hard, merciless joy of conquest, is disclosed by Turgenev in his rapid, yet exhaustive glances at her disdainful treatment of her many lovers, and of her cynical log of a husband. The extraordinarily clear light in the narrative, that of spring mountain air, waxes stronger towards the climax, and the artistic effort of the whole is that of some exquisite Greek cameo, with figures of centaurs and fleeing nymphs and youthful shepherds; though the postscript indeed is an excrescence which detracts from the main impression of pure, classic outlines.

Not less perfect as art though far slighter in scope is the exquisite *A Living Relic* (1874), one of the last of *A Sportsman's Sketches*. Along with the narrator we pass, in a step, from the clear sunlight and freshness of early morning, "when the larks' songs seemed steeped in dew," into the "little wattled shanty with its burden of a woman's suffering," poor Lukerya's, who lies, summer after summer, resigned to her living death:

> "... I was walking away....
>
> "'Master, master! Piotr Petrovitch!' I heard a voice, faint, slow, and hoarse, like the whispering of marsh rushes.
>
> "I stopped.

"'Piotr Petrovitch! Come in, please!' the voice repeated. It came from the corner where were the trestles I had noticed.

"I drew near, and was struck dumb with amazement. Before me lay a living human being; but what sort of creature was it?

"A head utterly withered, of a uniform coppery hue—like some very ancient and holy picture, yellow with age; a sharp nose like a keen-edged knife; the lips could barely be seen— only the teeth flashed white and the eyes; and from under the kerchief sometimes wisps of yellow hair struggled on to the forehead. At the chin, where the quilt was folded, two tiny hands of the same coppery hue were moving, the fingers slowly twitching like little sticks. I looked more intently; the face far from being ugly was positively beautiful, but strange and dreadful; and the face seemed more dreadful to me that on it—on its metallic cheeks—I saw struggling ... struggling and unable to form itself—a smile.

"'You don't recognize me, master?' whispered the voice again; it seemed to be breathed from the almost unmoving lips! 'And, indeed, how should you? I'm Lukerya.... Do you remember, who used to lead the dance at your mother's, at Spasskoe?... Do you remember, I used to be leader of the choir, too?'

"'Lukerya!' I cried. 'Is it you? Can it be?'

"'Yes, it's I, master—I, Lukerya.'

"I did not know what to say, and gazed in stupefaction at the dark motionless face with the clear, deathlike eyes fastened upon me. Was it possible? This mummy Lukerya—the greatest beauty in all our household—that tall, plump, pink-and-white, singing, laughing, dancing creature! Lukerya, our smart Lukerya, whom all our lads were courting, for whom I heaved some secret sighs—I a boy of sixteen!"

Lukerya tells her story. How one night she could not sleep, and, thinking of her lover, rose to listen to a nightingale in the garden; how half-dreaming she fell from the top stairs—and now she lives on, a little shrivelled mummy. Something is broken inside her body, and the doctors all shake their heads over her case. Her lover, Polyakov, has married another girl, a good sweet woman. "He couldn't stay a bachelor all his life, and they have children."

And Lukerya? All is not blackness in her wasted life. She is grateful for people's kindness to her.... She can hear everything, see everything that comes near her shed—the nesting swallows, the bees, the doves cooing on the roof. Lying alone in the long hours she can smell every scent from the garden, the flowering buckwheat, the lime tree. The priest, the peasant girls, sometimes a pilgrim woman, come and talk to her, and a little girl, a pretty, fair little thing, waits on her. She has her religion, her strange dreams, and sometimes, in her poor, struggling little voice that wavers like a thread of smoke, she tries to sing, as of old. But she is waiting for merciful death—which now is nigh her.

Infinitely tender in the depth of understanding is this gem of art, and *A Living Relic's* perfection is determined by Turgenev's scrutiny of the warp and woof of life, in which the impassive forces of Nature, indifferent alike to human pain or human happiness, pursue their implacable way, weaving unwittingly the mesh of joy, anguish, resignation, in the breast of all sentient creation. It is in the *spiritual perspective* of the picture, in the vision that sees the whole in the part, and the part in the whole, that Turgenev so far surpasses all his European rivals.

To those critics, Russian and English, who naïvely slur over the aesthetic qualities of a masterpiece, such as *A Lear of the Steppes* (1870), or fail to recognize all that aesthetic perfection implies, we address these concluding remarks. *A Lear of the Steppes* is great in art, because it is a living organic whole, springing from the deep roots of life itself; and the innumerable works of art that are fabricated and pasted together from an ingenious plan—works that do not grow from the inevitability of things—appear at once insignificant or false in comparison.

In examining the art, the artist will note Turgenev's method of introducing his story. Harlov, the Lear of the story, is brought forward with such force on the threshold that all eyes resting on his figure cannot but follow his after-movements. And absolute conviction gained, all the artist's artful after-devices and subtle presentations and side-lights on the story are not apparent under the straightforward ease and the seeming carelessness with which the narrator describes his boyish memories. Then the inmates of Harlov's household, his two daughters, and a crowd of minor characters, are brought before us as persons in the tragedy, and we see that all these people are living each from the innate laws of his being, apparently independently of the author's scheme. This conviction, that the author has no prearranged plan, convinces us that in the story we are living a piece of life: here we are verily plunging into life itself.

And the story goes on flowing easily and naturally till the people of the neighbourhood, the peasants, the woods and fields around, are known by us as intimately as is any neighbourhood in life. Suddenly a break—the tragedy is upon us. Suddenly the terrific forces that underlie human life, even the meanest of human lives, burst on us astonished and breathless, precisely as a tragedy comes up to the surface and bursts on us in real life: everybody runs about dazed, annoyed, futile; we watch other people sustaining their own individuality inadequately in the face of the monstrous new events which go their fatal way logically, events which leave the people huddled and useless and gasping. And destruction having burst out of life, life slowly returns to its old grooves—with a difference to us, the difference in the relation of people one to another that a death or a tragedy always leaves to the survivors. Marvellous in its truth is Turgenev's analysis of the situation after Harlov's death, marvellous is the simple description of the neighbourhood's attitude to the Harlov family, and marvellous is the lifting of the scene on the afterlife of Harlov's daughters. In the pages (pages 140, 141, 146, 147) on these women, Turgenev flashes into the reader's mind an extraordinary sense of the inevitability of these women's natures, of their innate growth fashioning their after-lives as logically as a beech puts out beech-leaves and an oak oak-leaves. Through Turgenev's single glimpse at their fortunes one knows the whole intervening fifteen years; he has carried us into a new world; yet it is the old world; one needs to know no more. It is life arbitrary but inevitable, life so clarified by art that it is absolutely interpreted; but life with all the sense of mystery that nature breathes around it in its ceaseless growth.

This sense of inevitability and of the mystery of life which Turgenev gives us in *A Lear of the Steppes* is the highest demand we can make from art. If we contrast with it two examples of Turgenev's more "romantic" manner, *Acia*, though it gives us a sense of mystery, is not inevitable: the end is *faked* to suit the artist's purpose, and thus, as in other ways, it is far inferior to *Lear*. *Faust* has consummate charm in its strange atmosphere of the supernatural mingling with things earthly, but it is not, as is *A Lear of the Steppes*, life seen from the surface to the revealed depths; it is a revelation of the strange forces in life, presented beautifully; but it is rather an idea, a problem to be worked out by certain characters, than a piece of life inevitable and growing. When an artist creates in us the sense of inevitability, then his work is at its highest, and is obeying Nature's law of growth, unfolding from out itself as inevitably as a tree or a flower or a human being unfolds from out itself. Turgenev at his highest never quits Nature, yet he always uses the surface, and what is apparent, to disclose her most secret principles, her deepest potentialities, her inmost laws of being, and whatever he presents he presents clearly and simply. This combination of powers marks only the few supreme artists. Even great masters often fail in perfect *naturalness*: Tolstoy's *The Death of Ivan Ilytch*, for instance, one of the most powerful stories ever written, has too little of what is typical of the whole of life, too much that is strained towards the general purpose of the story, to be perfectly *natural*. Turgenev's special feat in fiction is that his characters reveal themselves by the most ordinary details of their everyday life; and while these details are always giving us the whole life of the people, and their inner life as well, the novel's significance is being built up simply out of these details, built up by the same process, in fact, as Nature creates for us a single strong impression out of a multitude of little details.

Again, Turgenev's power as a poet comes in, whenever he draws a commonplace figure, to make it bring with it a sense of the mystery of its existence. In *Lear* the steward Kvitsinsky plays a subsidiary part; he has apparently no significance in the story, and very little is told about him. But who does not perceive that Turgenev looks at and presents the figure of this man in a manner totally different from the way any clever novelist of the second rank would look at and use him? Kvitsinsky, in Turgenev's hands, is an individual with all the individual's mystery in his glance, his coming and going, his way of taking things; but he is a part of the household's breath, of its very existence; he breathes the atmosphere naturally and creates an atmosphere of his own.

It is, then, in his marvellous sense of the growth of life that Turgenev is superior to most of his rivals. Not only did he observe life minutely and comprehensively, but he reproduced it as a constantly growing phenomenon, growing naturally, not accidentally or arbitrarily. For example, in *A House of Gentlefolk*, take Lavretsky's and Liza's changes of mood when they are falling in love with one another; it is Nature herself in them changing very delicately and insensibly; we feel that the whole picture is alive, not an effect cut out from life, and cut off from it at the same time, like a bunch of cut flowers, an effect which many clever novelists often give us. And in *Lear* we feel that the life in Harlov's village is still going on, growing yonder, still growing with all its mysterious sameness and changes, when, in Turgenev's last words, "The story-teller ceased, and we talked a little longer, and then parted, each to his home."

XI
NOTE ON TURGENEV'S LIFE

CHAPTER XI

Note on Turgenev's Life—His Character and Philosophy—*Enough* — *Hamlet and Don Quixote*—The *Poems in Prose*—Turgenev's last Illness and Death—His Epitaph.

If we have said nothing hitherto about the twenty years of Turgenev's life (1855-1877), in which the six great novels were composed, it is because his cosmopolitan activities, social, political, intellectual, were too many to be chronicled in the compass of a short Study. They may be here indicated in a few lines. Lengthy stays in France, and visits to Germany, Italy, England, were alternated with residence every year at Spasskoe. His attachment to Madame Viardot and her family (which may be studied in *Lettres à Madame Viardot*, Paris, 1907, a series unfortunately not published in its entirety) led to his joining their household at Courtavenel and Paris, and later (1864) to settling with them at Baden. His residence in France brought him into contact with nearly all the celebrated French men of letters, Mériemé, Taine, Renan, Victor Hugo, Sainte-Beuve, Flaubert, etc., and later with the chiefs of the young naturalistic school, as Zola, Daudet, Guy de Maupassant. Turgenev's political outlook and Liberal creed are best represented in his Correspondence with Hertzen, to whom he communicated Russian news for *The Bell*: his relations and quarrel with Tolstoy, and his enthusiastic appreciation of the latter's genius are recorded in Biriukoff's *Life of Tolstoy*, and in Halperine-Kaminsky's *Correspondence*. For his relations with Russian contemporary men of letters, Fet, Grigorovitch, Nekrassov, Dostoevsky, Annenkov, Aksakov, etc., there exists a mass of documents, letters and reminiscences in the Russian. For a general sketch of Turgenev's life the English reader can turn to E. Haumant's *Ivan Tourguéniéf*, Paris, 1906; for an account of Turgenev's youth, his relations with the Nihilists, his later life in Paris, etc., to Michel Delines' *Tourguénief Inconnu*, and also to the much-abused but valuable volume, *Souvenirs sur Tourguéneff*, by Isaac Pavlovsky.

All these sources reveal Turgenev in much the same light, a man of boundless cosmopolitan interests, of a broad, sane, fertile mind, of the most generous and tender heart. Some of his contemporaries touch on certain weaknesses, his vacillating will, his fits of hypochondria, his romantic affectation in youth, etc., but everybody bears witness (as does his Correspondence) to his lovableness, and the extraordinary altruism and sweetness of his nature. Thus Maupassant, a keen judge of character, records:

> "He was one of the most remarkable writers of this century, and at the same time the most honest, straightforward, universally sincere and affectionate man one could possibly meet. He was simplicity itself, kind and honest to excess,

> more good-natured than any one in the world, affectionate as men rarely are, and loyal to his friends whether living or dead.
>
> "No more cultivated, penetrating spirit, no more loyal, generous heart than his ever existed."

Such a man's philosophy can in no sense be termed "pessimistic," since the wells of his spirit are constantly fed by springs of understanding, love and charity. The whole body of Turgenev's work appeals to our faith in the ever-springing, renovating power of man's love of the good and the beautiful, and to his spiritual struggle with evil. But, faced by the threatening mass of wrong, of human stupidity and greed, of men's pettiness and blindness, Turgenev's beauty of feeling often recoils in a wave of melancholy and of sombre mournfulness. Thus in *Enough* (1864), a fragment inspired by the seas of acrimonious misunderstanding raised by *Fathers and Children*, Turgenev has concentrated in a prose poem of lyrical beauty, an access of profound dejection. Here we see laid bare the roots of Turgenev's philosophic melancholy,—man's insignificance in face of "the deaf, blind, dumb force of nature ... which triumphs not even in her conquests but goes onward, onward devouring all things.... She creates destroying, and she cares not whether she creates or she destroys.... How can we stand against those coarse and mighty waves, endlessly, unceasingly, moving upward? How have faith in the value and dignity of the fleeting images, that in the dark, on the edge of the abyss, we shape out of dust for an instant?" After recording many exquisite memories of nature and of love, Turgenev, then, compares human activities to those of gnats on the forest edge on a frosty day when the sun gleams for a moment: "At once the gnats swarm up on all sides; they sport in the warm rays, bustle, flutter up and down, circle round one another.... The sun is hidden—the gnats fall in a feeble shower, and there is the end of their momentary life. And men are ever the same." "What is terrible is that there is nothing terrible, that the very essence of life is petty, uninteresting and degradingly inane."

> "But are there no great conceptions, no great words of consolation: patriotism, right, freedom, humanity, art? Yes, those words there are and many men live by them and for them. And yet it seems to me that if Shakespeare could be born again he would have no cause to retract his Hamlet, his Lear. His searching glance would discover nothing new in human life: still the same motley picture—in reality so little complex—would unroll beside him in its terrifying sameness. The same credulity and the same cruelty, the same lust of blood, of gold, of filth, the same vulgar pleasures, the same senseless sufferings in the name ... why

in the name of the very same shams that Aristophanes jeered at two thousand years ago, the same coarse snares in which the many-headed beast, the multitude, is caught so easily, the same workings of power, the same traditions of slavishness, the same innateness of falsehood—in a word, the same busy squirrel's turning in the old, unchanged wheel...."

With this passage of weary disillusionment and disgust of life we may compare one in *Phantoms*, written a year earlier: "These human flies, a thousand times paltrier than flies; their dwellings glued together with filth, the pitiful traces of their tiny, monotonous bustle, of their comic struggle with the unchanging and inevitable, how revolting it all suddenly was to me"; and one, no less significant, in the opening pages of *The Torrents of Spring*:

"He thought of the vanity, the uselessness, the vulgar falsity of all things human.... Everywhere the same everlasting pouring of water into a sieve, the everlasting beating of the air, everywhere the same self-deception—half in good faith, half conscious—any toy to amuse the child, so long as it keeps him from crying. And then all of a sudden old age drops down like snow on the head, and with it the ever-growing, ever-growing and devouring dread of death ... and the plunge into the abyss."

But to show these waves of pessimistic exhaustion in right relation to the whole volume of Turgenev's work, one must contrast them with many hundreds of passages where the struggle of love, faith and courage, where the impulse of pity and beauty of conduct rank supreme in all human endeavour. And in his illuminating essay on *Hamlet and Don Quixote* (1860), Turgenev holds the balance level between humanity's blind faith in the power of the good (Don Quixote), and the disillusionment of its knowledge (Hamlet). Here Turgenev shows us that sincerity and force of conviction in the justice or goodness of a cause (however wrong-headed or absurd the idealist's judgment may be) is the prime basis for the pursuit of virtue, and that true enthusiasm for goodness and beauty exacts self-sacrifice, disregard of one's own interest, and forgetfulness of the "I." Hamlet by his sceptical intelligence becomes so conscious of his own weakness, of the worthlessness of the crowd, of the self-regarding motives of men, that he is unable to love them. Hence his irony, his melancholy, his despair in the triumph of the good, for which he, too, struggles, while paralysed by his thoughts which sap his will and condemn him to inactivity. "The Hamlets," says Turgenev, "find nothing, discover nothing, and leave no trace in their passage through the world but the memory of their personality: they have no spiritual legacy to bequeath. They do not love: they do not believe. How, then, should they find?"

Love and faith in the good and beautiful—based on forgetfulness of self—must therefore be set against and balance the rule of the intelligence, and this is precisely the effect Turgenev's work makes on us and the effect which his personality made on his acquaintances. "This man was all good," says Vogüé. "I think one would have to search the literary world for a long time before finding a writer capable of such modesty and such effacement," says Halpérine-Kaminsky. "I am always thinking about Turgenev. I love him terribly," says Tolstoy naïvely, after his lifelong hostility to Turgenev's genius had been removed by the latter's death. And all Turgenev's acquaintances agreed that no one was so devoid of egoism, so generous in his enthusiasm for the works of other men as he.[25] The guiding law of his being was shown not only in his unmeasured desire to exalt the works of his rivals,[26] but to find excellent, absorbing qualities in the works of obscure, unsuccessful writers. This trait often appeared, to his own circle, to be proof of mere uncritical misplaced enthusiasm, but in fact Turgenev was a most severe and impartial critic.[27] There is in even the humblest work of art, that is not false, a nucleus of individual feeling, experience, insight which cannot be replaced. And Turgenev, always searching for the good, instantly detected any individual excellence and emphasized its value, without dwelling on a work's mediocre elements. The world, and the generality of men, do exactly the reverse; they take pleasure in pointing out and publishing defects and weaknesses and in ignoring the points of strength.

[25] "On arriving at his rooms, Tourguéneff took from his writing-table a roll of paper. I give what he said word for word.

"'Listen,' he said. 'Here is "copy" for your paper of an absolutely first-rate kind. This means that I am not its author. The master—for he is a *real* master—is almost unknown in France, but I assure you, on my soul and conscience, that I do not consider myself worthy to unloose the latchet of his shoes.'

"Two days afterwards there appeared in the *Temps*, 'Les Souvenirs de Sebastopol,' by Leòn Tolstoi."—*Tourguéneff and his French Circle*, p. 188.

[26] "From the letters to Zola ... we shall see with what devotion, sparing neither time nor trouble, Tourguéneff endeavoured to make his friend's books known in Russia. What he did for Zola, he had already done for Gustave Flaubert; afterwards came Goncourt's turn and that of Guy de Maupassant. Never did he take such minute pains to safeguard his own interests, as those he took in the service of his friends."—*Tourguéneff and his French Circle*, by E. Halpérine-Kaminsky, p. 186.

[27] Flaubert writing to George Sand says, "What an auditor and what a critic is Turgenev! He has dazzled me by the profundity of his judgments. Ah! if all those who dabble in literary criticism could have heard him, what a lesson! Nothing escapes him. At the end of a piece of a hundred lines he remembers a feeble epithet."

The *Poems in Prose* (1878-1882), this exquisite collection of short, detached descriptions, scenes, memories, and dreams, yields a complete synthesis in brief of the leading elements in Turgenev's own temperament and philosophy. The *Poems in Prose* are unique in Russian literature, one may say unsurpassed for exquisite felicity of language, and for haunting, rhythmical beauty. Turgenev's characteristic, *the perfect fusion of idea and emotion*, takes shape here in æsthetic contours which challenge the antique. As with all poetry of a high order, the creative emotion cannot be separated from the imperishable form in which it is cast, and ten lines of the original convey what a lengthy commentary would fail to communicate. We therefore quote a translation of three of the *Prose Poems* from a version which, however careful, must inevitably fall short of the original:

"NECESSITAS-VIS-LIBERTAS

"A BAS-RELIEF

"A tall bony old woman, with iron face and dull fixed look, moves along with long strides, and, with an arm dry as a stick, pushes before her another woman.

"This woman—of huge stature, powerful, thickset, with the muscles of a Hercules, with a tiny head set on a bull neck, and blind—in her turn pushes before her a small, thin girl.

"This girl alone has eyes that see; she resists, turns round, lifts fair, delicate hands; her face full of life, shows impatience and daring.... She wants not to obey, she wants not to go, where they are driving her ... but, still, she has to yield and go.

"*Necessitas-vis-Libertas!*

"Who will, may translate."

"THE SPARROW

"I was returning from hunting, and walking along an avenue of the garden, my dog running in front of me. Suddenly he took shorter steps, and began to steal along as though tracking game.

"I looked along the avenue and saw a young sparrow, with yellow about its beak and down on its head. It had fallen out of the nest (the wind was violently shaking the birch-trees in the avenue) and sat unable to move, helplessly fluffing its half-grown wings.

"My dog was slowly approaching it, when, suddenly darting down from a tree close by, an old dark-throated sparrow fell like a stone right before its nose, and all ruffled up, terrified, with despairing and pitiful cheeps, it flung itself twice toward the open jaws of shining teeth.

"It sprang to save; it cast itself before its nestling ... but all its tiny body was shaking with terror; its note was harsh and strange. Swooning with fear it offered itself up!

"What a huge monster must the dog have seemed to it! And yet it could not stay on its high branch out of danger.... A force stronger than its will flung it down.

"My Trésor stood still, drew back.... Clearly he, too, recognized this force.

"I hastened to call off the disconcerted dog, and went away, full of reverence.

"Yes; do not laugh. I felt reverence for that tiny, heroic bird, for its impulse of love.

"Love, I thought, is stronger than death, or the fear of death. Only by it, by love, life holds together and advances."

The content, the quiet, the plenty of the Russian earth, "The Country"; the insignificance of man, "A Conversation"; there is no escape from death, "The Old Woman"; the tie between man and the animals, "The Dog"; death reconciles old enemies, "The Last Meeting"; Nature's indifference to man, "Nature"; the beauty of untroubled, innocent youth, "How Fair and Fresh were the Roses"; the genius of poesy, "A Visit"; the joy of giving and taking, "Alms"; the rich misjudge the poor, "Cabbage Soup"; we always pray for miracles, "Prayer"; Christ is in all men, "Christ"; the immortal hour of genius, "Stay"; love and hunger, "The Two Brothers"; such are a few of the subjects of the *Poems in Prose*. The permanent appeal of these exquisite little pieces lies in their soft, deep humanity and emotional freshness, while æsthetically they are marked by the broad warm touch in which Turgenev indicates the infinite lights and tones of living nature. Turgenev's supremacy in style rests, indeed, precisely here, in this faculty of concentrating in a few broad sweeping touches, a wealth of tones which, producing an individual effect, makes a universal appeal to feeling. It is mysterious, this faculty of so massing and concentrating your effect that one detailed touch does the work of half a dozen. Turgenev alone among his contemporaries had mastered this secret of Greek art. It is the emotional breadth, imparted in ease, sureness, and flexibility of stroke, that distinguishes the *Poems in Prose* from all other examples of the genre. Fresh as the rain, soft as the petal of a flower, warm as the touch of love is "The Rose," so simple, yet so complete in its message.

"THE ROSE

"The last days of August.... Autumn was already at hand.

"The sun was setting. A sudden downpour of rain, without thunder or lightning, had just passed rapidly over our wide plain.

"The garden in front of the house glowed and steamed, all filled with the fire of the sunset and the deluge of rain.

"She was sitting at a table in the drawing-room, and with persistent dreaminess, gazing through the half-open door into the garden.

"I knew what was passing at that moment in her soul; I knew that, after a brief but agonising struggle, she was at that instant giving herself up to a feeling she could no longer master.

"All at once she got up, went quickly out into the garden, and disappeared.

"An hour passed ... a second; she had not returned.

"Then I got up, and, going out of the house, I turned along the walk by which—of that I had no doubt—she had gone.

"All was darkness about me; the night had already fallen. But on the damp sand of the path a roundish object could be discerned—bright red even through the mist.

"I stooped down. It was a fresh, new-blown rose. Two hours before I had seen this very rose on her bosom.

"I carefully picked up the flower that had fallen in the mud, and, going back to the drawing-room, laid it on the table before her chair.

"And now at last she came back, and with light footsteps, crossing the whole room, sat down at the table.

"Her face was both paler and more vivid; her downcast eyes, that looked somehow smaller, strayed rapidly in happy confusion from side to side.

"She saw the rose, snatched it up, glanced at its crushed, muddy petals, glanced at me, and her eyes, brought suddenly to a standstill, were bright with tears.

"'What are you crying for?' I asked.

"'Why, see this rose. Look what has happened to it.'

"Then I thought fit to utter a profound remark.

"'Your tears will wash away the mud,' I pronounced with a significant expression.

"'Tears do not wash, they burn,' she answered. And turning to the hearth she flung the rose into the dying flame.

"'Fire burns even better than tears,' she cried with spirit; and her lovely eyes, still bright with tears, laughed boldly and happily.

"I saw that she, too, had been through the fire."

A few of the *Poems in Prose*, profoundly ironical, as "The Fool," "A Contented Man," "The Egoist," "A Rule of Life," "Two Strangers," "The Workmen and the Man with the White Hands," show the indignation of a large generous heart with human baseness, pettiness, stupidity, and envy. A minority of the poems are instinct with Turgenev's morbid apprehension of death's stealthy approach, and the final, unescapable blotting out of life and love by his clutch. Turgenev's dread of the malignant forces of decay and dissolution had found powerful expression nearly twenty years earlier in *Phantoms*, where a series of prose poems is enshrined in the setting of a story.

"'Do not utter her name, not her name,' Alice faltered hurriedly. 'We must escape, or there will be an end to everything and for ever.... Look over there!'

"I turned my head in the direction in which her trembling hand was pointing and discerned something ... horrible indeed.

"This something was the more horrible since it had no definite shape. Something bulky, dark, yellowish-black, spotted like a lizard's belly, not a storm-cloud, and not smoke, was crawling with a snakelike motion over the earth. A wide rhythmic undulating movement from above downwards, and from below upwards, an undulation recalling the malignant sweep of the wings of a vulture seeking its prey; at times an indescribably revolting grovelling on the earth, as of a spider stooping over its captured fly.... Who are you, what are you, menacing mass? Under its influence I saw it, I felt it—all sank into nothingness, all was dumb.... A putrefying, pestilential chill came from it. At this chill breath the heart turned sick and the eyes grew dim, and the hair stood up on the head. It was a power moving; that power which there is no resisting, to which all is subject, which, sightless, shapeless, senseless, sees all, knows all, and like a bird of prey, picks out its victims, stifles them and stabs them with its frozen sting."

This passage, by the intensity of horror it evokes, shows how deeply entwined in the roots of Turgenev's joy in life was his loathing of death; and the same note is struck with cumulative force in "The End of the World" and "The Insect," where the chill atmosphere of frozen terror and suffocating dread is enforced by the gloomy imagery. There can be no doubt that Turgenev's premonitory obsession of death in his last years was one of the manifestations of the malignant disease of which he died—cancer of the spinal marrow—which cast the darkening shadow of melancholy over his vital energies and intensified his sensation of spiritual isolation. In the struggle between his healthy instincts and the weariness and dejection diffused by this creeping, malignant cancer, his latter days may be likened to those of an autumnal landscape at evening, with the valleys shivering in the shadows of approaching night, while the higher ground remains still flushed with warm light. But the *Poems in Prose*, his last work, declare how comparatively little the morbid processes at work within his frame had impaired his serene intelligence, his wide unflinching vision, his deep generous heart, and passion to help others. This, although he had already written, "I have grown old, all seems tarnished around me and within me. The light which rays from the heart, showing life in its colour, in relief, in movement, this light is nearly extinguished within me: it flickers under the crust of cinders which grows thicker and thicker." But his cruel malady in the last two years, when Turgenev endured "all that one can endure without dying," did not embitter his character.[28] Pavlovsky tells us:

"After terrible sufferings, during which the sick man could neither sit nor remain standing nor lying down, his condition improved. He could work and read free from pain, except when he moved about. That gave him hope that with many precautions, he would live a few years longer. But very soon a fresh access arrived, followed with fresh prostration of spirit.

"'When my sufferings are unendurable,' said Turgenev, 'I follow Schopenhauer's advice. I analyse my sensations and my agony departs for a period. For example, if my sufferings are terrible I can easily tell myself of what kind they are. First there is a stinging pain which, in itself, is not insupportable. To this is added a burning feeling, and next a shooting pang; then a difficulty in breathing. Separately each one is endurable and when I analyse them thus, it is easy for me to endure them. One must always do this in life, if you analyse your sufferings you will not suffer so much.'

"On another occasion he said to me:

"'I do not regret dying. I have had all the pleasures I could wish for. I have done much work. I have had success. I have loved people; and they have, also, loved me. I have reached old age. I have been as happy as one can be. Many have not had that. It is bad to die before the time comes, but for me it is time.'

"One need not say that these words were those of a sick man wishing to console himself. Turgenev knew well that he could still create, and he did not wish to die.

"In speaking of the condition of Viardot, who was also dying, Turgenev said to me:

"'A bad thing this death! One couldn't complain if she killed one at a stroke; then it would be over; but she glides behind you like a robber, takes from man all his soul, his intelligence, his love of the beautiful; she attacks the essence of the human being. The envelope alone remains.'

"And he added, after a moment's silence, in a whisper, strangely passionate:

"'Yes, death is the lie!' ...

"A thing strange and most characteristic was that during his last illness Turgenev never ceased to occupy himself with the affairs of others.... Moreover, he did not wait to be solicited to render people services."

[28] *Ossip Lourié*, p. 63.

In his last days Turgenev addressed to Tolstoy the famous letter in which he adjured him to return to literature,[29] and bequeathed to others as his creed and example his farewell words, "Live and love others as I have always loved them." After renewed cruel sufferings he sank into a delirium, and died at Bougival on September 3, 1883. Madame Viardot describes his end, thus:

"He had lost consciousness since two days. He no longer suffered, his life slowly ebbed away, and after two convulsions, he breathed his last. He looked as beautiful again as ever. On the first day after death, there was still a deep wrinkle, caused by the convulsions, between his eyebrows; the second day his habitual expression of goodness reappeared. One would have expected to see him smile."[30]

[29] "Kind and dear Leo Nikoláyevitch,—I have long not written to you, because, to tell the truth, I have been, and am, on my deathbed. I cannot recover: that is out of the question, I am writing to you specially to say how glad I am to be your contemporary, and to express my last and sincere request. My friend, return to literary activity! That gift came to you whence comes all the rest. Ah! how happy I should be if I could think my request would have an effect on you!... I am played out—the doctors do not even know what to call my malady, *névralgie stomacale goutteuse*. I can neither walk, nor eat, nor sleep. It is wearisome even to repeat it all! My friend—great writer of our Russian land—listen to my request!... I can write no more I am tired. (Unsigned), Bougival, 27 or 28 June 1883."—Translated by A. Maude, *The Life of Tolstoy*, vol. ii. p. 182.

[30] For this and other details, see Haumant, p. 110.

The autopsy made by the French doctors revealed that the weight of Turgenev's brain, 2012 grammes, surpassed by a third the normal weight, and, though Turgenev's high stature partly accounted for this, the doctors were astonished by its volume, which much exceeded Cuvier's, hitherto the largest brain known.

Turgenev was buried, according to his wish, in the Volkov cemetery at Petersburg, by the side of his friend, the critic Byelinsky. A crowd of 100,000 people accompanied the funeral procession, including 285 deputations from all parts of Russia. The Russian Government declined to take part in it![31] Renan, in France, pronounced the valedictory oration, and the passage we extract stands as Turgenev's noble epitaph:

> "Au-dessus de la race, en effect, il y a l'humanité, ou, si l'on veut, la raison. Tourguéneff fut d'une race par sa manière de sentir et de peindre; il appartenait à l'humanité tout entière par une haute philosophie, envisageant d'un œil ferme les conditions de l'existence humaine et cherchant

sans parti pris à savoir la réalité. Cette philosophie aboutissait chez lui à la douceur, à la joie de vivre, à la pitié pour les créatures, pour les victimes surtout. Cette pauvre humanité souvent aveugle assurément, mais si souvent aussi trahie par ses chefs, il l'aimait ardemment. Il applaudissait à son effort spontané vers le bien et le vrai. Il ne gourmandait pas ses illusions; il ne lui en voulait pas de se plaindre. La politique de fer qui raille ceux qui souffrent n'était pas la sienne. Aucune déception ne l'arrêtait. Comme l'univers, il eut recommencé mille fois l'œuvre manquée; il savait que la justice peut attendre; on finira toujours par y revenir. Il avait vraiment les paroles de la vie éternelle, les paroles de paix, de justice, d'amour et de liberté."

[31] On Turgenev's death, Lavrov, the Russian refugee, stated that Turgenev had contributed 500 francs annually to the expenses of the revolutionary Zurich paper *En Avant*. The Russian Government hastened to manifest its displeasure accordingly.

THE END

Milton Keynes UK
Ingram Content Group UK Ltd.
UKHW030909151124
451262UK00006B/874